EMERGENCE

LABELED

AUTISTIC

Temple Grandin
and
Margaret M. Scariano

Updated References (1993)

ISBN: 0-87879-524-3

2 1 0 9 8 7 6 5 4
7 6 5 4 3 2 1 0 9

Personal communications to Temple Grandin should be sent directly to 2918 Silver Plume Drive, Unit C3, Fort Collins, CO 80526 (303) 229-0703.

Translations of this book are available in Danish, German, Icelandic, Japanese and Swedish. Contact publisher for more information.

Contents

*Dedicated to my family
with love*

Foreword

Reading this book will be an adventure. There is no other book like it — even remotely like it. The reason is simple. The author has a story to tell, a true story, by the way, that is so breathtakingly unusual that it will be taken by many to be mere fiction. But it is true.

I first met Temple Grandin (that is her real name) almost twelve years ago. She had phoned to say that she had read my book *Infantile Autism* and wanted to visit me to discuss certain matters. She explained that she was a recovered autistic person and was now in college majoring in psychology. In recent years autism has become fashionable, and the term is vastly overused. Only about one-fourth of the people who tell me that they are recovered autistics seem to me to be probably correct. In Temple's case, her voice and her unusually direct manner persuaded me that she was a recovered (or recovering) autistic, but the content of her message made me skeptical. Very few autistic persons even manage to enter high school, and fewer still manage to make their way into college. Those who do usually major in math or computers, not psychology. And here she was, telephoning and planning to visit another city on her own. Such competence is extremely rare in autistic persons, and the initiative required by such activities is even rarer.

When she arrived, a tall, angular young lady, obsessed with squeeze machines and cattle chutes (yes, squeeze machines and cattle chutes—read the book!) I was convinced that she had diagnosed herself correctly. (When I agreed to write this foreword, I didn't realize how hard it would be. There is much to say, but saying it will give away the author's story, which I refuse to do, and may ruin your fun as well. Well, anyway . . .)

Temple's story of her childhood memories fascinated me, as they will you in the chapters that follow. Her scientific work was also fascinating. She hungered for knowledge, as any scientist does, but in her case the hunger was more intense since she was also trying to understand herself. Her choice of a career amazed me, and the recognition she had achieved in that career, even as a college student, was very impressive. It was a memorable meeting.

After talking a while, my wife and I took Temple out to lunch. Her loud, unmodulated voice (very characteristic of autistic persons) brought puzzled stares from the other diners, so I risked offending her by asking her several times to lower her voice. Wonder of wonders! She wasn't the slightest bit offended. Here was an individual who recognized that she had oddities and peculiarities of speech and manner as a result of her affliction with autism, but who took them as a matter of course, and regarded them as obstacles to be overcome, rather than reasons to be self-conscious or embarrassed. That same openness, candor, and just plain rational objectivity makes her book such good and informative reading. It is an unusual pleasure to deal with a person so forthright and uninterested in guile.

The part of my book that had captured Temple's attention and had led her to visit me was a small section in which I had commented on what appeared to be unusual reactions to touch on the part of a number of autistic children. This topic had been virtually ignored in the research literature on autism. Very little is known about the phenomenon, and it hardly seemed worthy of mention except that I had seen it referred to briefly in so many case histories that it occurred to me that there might be some much deeper underlying significance to this matter than had heretofore been recognized. As it turned out, Temple, because of her own circumstances, had become intensely interested in the topic and wanted to know if I had been able to learn more about the matter in the years that had passed since my book was published. I had learned a little more, not as much as I would have liked, and I shared my thoughts and ideas with Temple. As you will see, she has carried these ideas very far.

To my knowledge, this is the first book written by a recovered autistic individual. It is an exciting book. The reader shares the adventure of growing from an extremely handicapped child who appeared to be destined for permanent institutionalization to a vigorous, productive, and respected adult who is a world-authority in her field. Temple's ability to convey to the reader her innermost feelings and fears, coupled with her capacity for explaining her mental processes, will give the reader an insight into autism that very few have been able to achieve.

On speaking with Temple again recently, after a lapse of several years, I was impressed with how much less autistic-sounding she is today than she was when I first met her. She has continued to grow and develop. She has accomplished a great deal not only in her profession, but also in her avocation which is represented by this book. She has also accomplished a great deal as a human being. The indomitable spirit which shines through the pages of this book makes one proud to be human.

Bernard Rimland, PhD
Institute for Child Behavior Research
San Diego, California

Preface

What a rare pleasure for a teacher! To see a student after so many years. To know she's pursued her dreams against formidable odds and come out of it an impressive human being. And become a world authority in what she's chosen to do. And that she's written a book to ease the way for others. What a pleasure!

The headmaster of our school had asked me to talk to Temple. According to the staff, she was talking strangely and was asking very odd questions. He was concerned and wanted an opinion. (She was clearly one of his favorites.)

That was my first meeting with Temple. Her eye-to-eye directness, forcefulness, intensity, and strong handshake were not what would be expected from a typical adolescent. She was neat and clean, but put as little effort as possible into keeping up with current school fashion in clothes and hair; her interests were obviously elsewhere. In her no-nonsense voice, she wanted answers. I talked with her for several hours, much longer than I'd expected to do. Most of the strange talk and odd questions, it seemed to me, simply anticipated College Philosophy 101. And I found myself being pulled into her fascinating world of cattle chutes and becalmed calves.

The last time I saw Temple was some twenty years later while this book was in preparation. There was a striking similarity to our first meeting. Some of her original autistic qualities were still there, but were redirected — or even put to good use: her intense involvement in her doctoral research in animal psychophysiology; her still strong handshake; her functional Western clothes; her adamant resistance (relayed to me) to her mother's suggestion that her hair be "redone." Clearly, Temple hadn't emerged from autism by becoming a different person, but had taken and reworked what she already had.

Temple was involved in everything at school — from academic classes to carpentry to lock-picking. Her insistence on and persistence in getting an answer to her questions (most of them good, but difficult), her intense, often bizarre behavior, and unconventional boyish dress added up as a whole to respect but not social acceptance by most of the staff and students.

For all her unsocial behavior, Temple worried hard and long about what people thought of her. She worked constantly, trying to arrive at workable rules that dealt with her own and others' behavior. She was developing a fine ethical sense. I remember particularly her understanding when I gave an award in a model rocketry program to a boy for whom this was a major accomplishment rather than to Temple, who actually accomplished more.

Perhaps the most difficult barrier for Temple was the cruel kindness that wanted to protect her from expectations that might shatter because of her autism. The school, as a whole, expected, at best, that she might do well at a trade school because of her interest in carpentry. But Temple's intense focus was on the psychology of the cattle chute. And it was there that she found her way out of autism.

Temple has demonstrated, without question, that there is hope for the autistic child — that deep, constant caring, understanding, acceptance, appropriately high expectations, and support and encouragement for what is best in him will provide a base, from which he can grow to his own potential.

It will be easy to see, in this book, that I had an effect on Temple. What will not be so obvious is her effect on me. I watched her work with her autism, sometimes in the midst of extreme discouragement and confusion, and saw her come to terms with it. I know I've seen the human spirit at its best.

You will, too, as you read her book.

William Carlock
Educator
Berry Creek, California

Introduction

I put the announcement down and poured myself another cup of tea. Mountain Country School in Vermont was having a class reunion. Swarms of memories buzzed in my head.

Good old Mountain Country School . . . and dear Mr. Peters, the founder. Was my invitation to attend a mistake? Had someone forgotten that "bizarre kid," "that fixated nerd," "the weirdo who hit the other kids on the head"?

How could they forget? I *was* a "bizarre kid." I didn't even talk until I was three and a half years old. Until that time, screaming, peeping, humming were my means of communication. You see, I was labeled autistic. In 1943 Kanner developed the term "autism" to label the variety of symptoms. Several years later, I was evaluated as being autistic.

Over the years I have read enough to know that there are still many parents, and, yes, professionals, too, who believe that "once autistic, always autistic." This dictum has meant sad and sorry lives for many children diagnosed, as I was in early life, as autistic. To these people it is incomprehensible that the characteristics of autism can be modified and controlled. However, I feel strongly that I am living proof that they can. And this seems to be especially true of autistic children who have meaningful language skills before the age of five.

Today I am in my late thirties. I am a successful livestock handling equipment designer, one of very few in the world. I am called upon by firms throughout the world to advise and consult and to design special equipment for them. I contribute regularly to the professional journals in my field and speak at professional conferences across the country. Presently, I am completing my Ph.D. in Animal Science. My life is normal and totally independent with no financial worries.

How is it possible that a young child whose parents were told she might have to live her life in an institution can confound the "experts"? How does a child, labeled autistic, emerge into the real world? I still have some problem in relating to people. But I am surviving and coping with the world.

First of all, what is autism?

Autism is a developmental disorder. A defect in the systems which process incoming sensory information causes the child to over-react to some stimuli and under-react to others. The autistic child often withdraws from her environment and the people in it to block out an onslaught of incoming stimulation. Autism is a childhood anomaly that separates the child from interpersonal relationships. She does not reach out and explore the world around her, but instead stays in her own inner world. As I describe my memories in succeeding chapters, you will see how overly reactive I was to smells, movements, spinning, and sounds, as many other autistic children are. And how simple little movements could result in perseveration (behavior in which a person is unable to stop an activity once it is started, even when he wants to do so) which drove the adults around me to distraction.

What causes autism? Therein lies a mystery. Is it neurological? Is it physiological? Intrauterine trauma, rejection by the mother, or a lack of trace minerals? Is it brain damage? Is it psychogenic? The opinions of many eminent professionals vary. Research indicates that certain parts of the central nervous system may not develop properly. For some unknown reason the many millions of neurons which are growing in the developing brain make some wrong connections. Studies on the brains of deceased dyslexics, a condition that may be related to autism, indicate that neurons may have grown in the wrong directions. Research on autistics with sophisticated CAT and PET scanners indicate that some autistics have defects in neural development and some areas of the brain may be over-active. But the fact is that the symptoms, regardless of their form of autism, remain the same.

These symptoms seem to surface in the first few months of life. The infant does not respond like other babies. She isn't deaf because she reacts to sounds. Her reactions to other sensory stimuli are inconsistent. The smell of a rose plucked from the garden can throw the youngster into a tantrum — or cause her to retreat into her inner world. Other symptoms of autism are avoidance of being touched, lack of meaningful speech, repetitive behavior, temper tantrums, sensitivity to loud or unusual noises, and lack of emotional contact with people.

So, what are the treatments? Pick one — any one — sensory stimulation, behavior modification, education, drug treatment, diet, nutritional supplements. They've all been tried, and each has had some measure of success. Some autistics appear to respond to one and others to another. And some autistics require lifelong institutional care because of their lack of awareness of the world "out there" or their violent behavior.

My story is different and I offer hope to parents and professionals who deal with autistics because I was labeled autistic. Some clinicians may look at Mother's notes in my story and say that there is too much "normal" behavior — that I was misdiagnosed. Marion Sigman and Peter Mundy at UCLA in Los Angeles found that autistic children have more socially related behaviors than many people realize. When compared to matched controls of normal and retarded children, autistics obeyed their mother's commands as readily as the other two groups. To say that an autistic child has absolutely no response to people is a misconception. Lorna Wing at the Institute of Psychiatry in London states that an autistic child may be socially responsive in one situation but not in another. Autistic children are as varied in their skills, intelligence, likes and dislikes, social graces as "normal" children. In 1950 I was labeled autistic and groped my way from the far side of darkness.

As I was writing this book, I sent copies out to a wide range of specialists in child development and autism. It was interesting to get the feedback. Some of it said, in so many words, "But why weren't you in _____ therapy? That would have helped you." The problem is that thirty years ago, if _____ therapy had existed, only a small number of specialists knew about it. Remember, even the term "autism" had just been coined when I was a small child. A lot of what is now known simply wasn't available to the general public, much less the experts, thirty years ago.

Today my childhood memories are like a rich tapestry. I can still picture some parts of the fabric quite well. Other parts are faded. The incidents I recall tell a fascinating story on how autistic children perceive and

15

respond in unusual ways to the strange world around them — the world they are desperately trying to give some order to.

CHAPTER ONE

Childhood Memories

I remember the day I almost killed my mother and younger sister, Jean.

Mother had slid in behind the wheel of the car. Reaching over the back seat, she said, "Here's your hat, Temple. You want to look nice when you see the speech therapist, don't you?" She pulled the blue corduroy hat down over my ears, turned around and started the engine.

My ears felt as if they were being squashed together into one giant ear. The band of the hat pressed tightly around my head. I jerked the hat off and screamed. Screaming was my only way of telling Mother that I didn't want to wear the hat. It hurt. It smothered my hair. I hated it. I wouldn't wear it to "talking" school.

At the stop sign Mother turned around and looked at me. "Put that hat back on," she ordered and pulled onto the freeway.

I fingered the painful hat, trying to rub away the walls of the fabric. Humming tunelessly, I massaged the material over and over. Now the hat lay in my lap like an ugly blue blob. I had to get rid of it. I decided to throw it out the window. Mother wouldn't notice. She was too busy driving. But at a little over three years old, I couldn't crank my window down. Now the hat felt hot and prickly on my lap. It lay there waiting, like a monster. Impulsively I leaned forward and tossed it out Mother's window.

She yelled. I covered my ears to shut out the hurting sound. She made a grab for the hat. The car swerved. Suddenly we were jolting into the other lane. I leaned back against the seat and enjoyed the jostling. Jean was in the back seat crying. Even today I remember the bushes planted along the highway. I close my eyes and feel again the warm sun streaming in the window, smell the exhaust fumes and see the red tractor-trailer truck come closer and closer.

Mother tried to turn the wheel, but it was too late. I heard the crush of metal and felt a violent jolt as we sideswiped the red tractor-trailer truck and suddenly stopped. I yelled, "Ice. Ice. Ice," as broken glass showered all over me. I was not scared at all. It was kind of exciting.

The side of the car was bashed in. It was a miracle I hadn't killed us all. It also was sort of a miracle that I had been able to get the word "ice" out clearly and succinctly. As an autistic child, difficulty in speaking was one of my greatest problems. Although I could understand everything people said, my responses were limited. I'd try, but most of the time no spoken words came. It was similar to stuttering; the words just wouldn't come out. Yet, there were times when I said words like "ice" quite clearly. This often occurred during a stressful period such as the car accident when stress overcame the barrier which usually prevented me from speaking. This is just one of the puzzling, frustrating, confusing things about childhood autism that drives adults to distraction. People around me wondered why I could talk at one time and not another. Maybe I wasn't trying or I was spoiled. Then they'd be even harder on me.

Perhaps, because of my inability to communicate adequately and because of my "inner" world, the scenes of my childhood are vivid. Memories play like a movie on the big screen of my mind.

Mother, who was only nineteen when I was born, said she remembers me as a normal, healthy newborn with big blue eyes, a mass of downy brown hair, and a dimple in my chin. A quiet, "good" baby girl named Temple.

If I could remember those first days and weeks of life, would I have known I was on a fast slide slipping into an abyss of aloneness? Cut off by over-reactions or inconsistent reactions from my five senses? Would I have sensed the alienation I would experience because of brain damage suffered as an unborn child—the brain damage that would become apparent in life when that part of the damaged brain matured?

I was six months old when Mother noticed that I was no longer cuddly and that I stiffened up when she held me. When I was a few months older, Mother tried to gather me into her arms, and I clawed at her like a trapped animal. She has said she didn't understand my behavior and felt hurt by my hostile actions. She'd seen other babies cuddling and cooing in their mother's arms. What was *she* doing wrong? But she figured she was young and inexperienced. Having an autistic child was scary for her because she didn't know how to respond towards a baby who rejected her. Maybe my seeming rejection was not unusual so she shoved her apprehension aside. After all, my health was good. I was alert, intelligent, and well-coordinated. Since I was the first-born,

Mother thought my withdrawal was probably normal, part of maturing and becoming independent.

This withdrawal from touch, so typical of autistic children, was followed in the next years by standard autistic behaviors: my fixation on spinning objects, my preference to be alone, destructive behavior, temper tantrums, inability to speak, sensitivity to sudden noises, appearance of deafness, and my intense interest in odors.

I was a destructive child. I drew all over the walls — not once or twice — but any time I got my hands on a pencil or crayon. I remember really "catching" it for peeing on the carpet. So the next time I had to go, instead of using the carpet, I put the long drape between my legs. I thought it would dry quickly and Mother wouldn't notice. Normal children use clay for modeling; I used my feces and then spread my creations all over the room. I chewed up puzzles and spit the cardboard mush out on the floor. I had a violent temper, and when thwarted, I'd throw anything handy — a museum quality vase or leftover feces. I screamed continually, responded violently to noise and yet appeared deaf on some occasions.

At age three Mother took me to a neurologist to be examined because I did not act like the little girls next door. I was the first child in a family of four and none of my younger sisters or brothers behaved the way I did.

The EEG and hearing tests were normal. I was measured on the Rimland checklist where a score of +20 indicates classical autism (Kanner's syndrome). I scored +9. (Only about 10 percent of children described as autistic fit in the narrowly defined Kanner's syndrome because there are metabolic differences between Kanner's syndrome and other types of autism.) Although my behavior patterns were definitely autistic, the beginnings of basic, infantile but nonetheless meaningful sounds by age three and one half lowered my Rimland checklist score. But the frustration for both parent and child is evident in any degree of autism. After the evaluation, the doctor said there was no physical impairment. He suggested a speech therapist for my communication disability.

Up to this time, communication had been a one-way street for me. I could understand what was being said, but I was unable to respond. Screaming and flapping my hands was my only way to communicate. Mrs. Reynolds was the speech therapist and except for her use of a pointer, I have warm memories of her. But I was scared of her pointer. The stick was sharp and wicked-looking. I'd been drilled at home never to point a sharp object at anyone. It could poke out an eye. Now Mrs. Reynolds was pointing it at me! I shrank back in fear. I don't believe she ever understood my terror of that stick. And I wasn't able to explain my fear to her. In spite of this one negative aspect, Mrs. Reynolds helped me. It was here that I answered the telephone for the first time. Mrs. Reynolds had stepped out of the room for a moment. The telephone rang. And rang. And rang. No one answered it. The irritation and stress of the sound of that telephone jangling seemed to break through the barrier of my usual pattern of stuttering words. I ran across the room and picked up the receiver and said, "Hul-lo!" Alexander Graham Bell's first call couldn't have had more of a stunned reaction.

Mother said at first I had a very limited vocabulary and stressed words heavily like "bah" for ball. I spoke in a one word pattern — "ice," "go," "mine," "no." My efforts must have sounded wonderful to Mother. What a step forward from humming, peeping, and squealing!

But it wasn't only my lack of speech that concerned Mother. My voice was flat with little inflection and no rhythm. That alone stamped me as different. Coupled with speech difficulty and lack of voice inflection, I was well into adulthood before I could look people in the eye. As a child I remember Mother asking me time and again, "Temple, are you listening to me? Look at me." Sometimes I wanted to, but couldn't. Darting eyes — so characteristic of many autistic children — was another symptom of my autistic behavior. There were other tell-tale signs. I had little interest in other children, preferring my own inner world. I could sit on the beach for hours dribbling sand through my fingers and fashioning miniature mountains. Each particle of sand intrigued me as though I were a scientist looking through a microscope. Other times I scrutinized each line in my finger, following one as if it were a road on a map.

Spinning was another favorite activity. I'd sit on the floor and twirl around. The room spun with me. This self-stimulatory behavior made me feel powerful, in control of things. After all, I could make a whole room turn around. Sometimes I made the world spin by twisting the swing in our backyard so that the chains would wind up. Then I'd sit there as the swing unwound, watching the sky and earth whirl. I realize that non-autistic children enjoy twirling around in a swing, too. The difference is the autistic child is obsessed with the act of spinning.

There is a mechanism in the inner ear that controls the body's balance and integrates visual and vestibular input. Through a series of nerve connections, the eyes, after some amount of spinning, will start jumping about (become nystagmatic) and the stomach queasy. Then, the child will stop twirling or spinning. Autistic children often have reduced nystagmus. It is as if their bodies were demanding more spinning as a kind of corrective factor in an immature nervous system.

Whatever the reason, I enjoyed twirling myself around or spinning coins or lids round and round and round. Intensely preoccupied with the movement of the spinning coin or lid, I saw nothing or heard nothing. People around me were transparent. And no sound intruded on my fixation. It was as if I were deaf. Even a sudden loud noise didn't startle me from my world.

But when I was in the world of people, I was extremely sensitive to noises. Every summer we went to the family vacation place at Nantucket. This involved a forty-five minute trip on the ferry. I hated this part of the trip. What was exciting and adventuresome to Mother and my younger sisters and brother was a nightmare of sound to me, violating my ears and very soul.

Mother and our governess insisted we sit on the deck. "Just smell the nice fresh air, children," Mother would say.

"Healthy air! It'll put apples in those cheeks for sure," the governess always added.

The only problem was that to get the nice, healthy, apple-putting air in our cheeks, we had to sit directly under the fog horn. The pain that racked my head when the fog horn sounded was excruciating. Even with my hands over my ears the hurtful sound assaulted them to the point that I'd throw myself down on the deck and scream.

"Poor Temple! She's not much of a sailor," Mother said.

I can still see the governess' lips tightened in disgust at Mother's naiveté. She knew. Miss Cray was a typical old maid. She had grey hair worn in a bun on the back of her head. Whalebone pins, which I thought went straight into her scalp, held the bun secure. She always wore smocks that made her look like a French painter. She had many fine qualities and gave my sister, Jean, and me her undivided attention. She played games with us, took us sledding, and played the piano so we could march around the room. But she didn't believe in frivolous hugging. She never touched us unless it was to punish us. Now, years later, I know Miss Cray sensed my distress of loud noises. Such sounds not only startle autistic children but cause them intense discomfort.

Like birthday parties. They were torture for me. The confusion created by noise-makers suddenly going off startled me. I would invariably react by hitting another child or by picking up an ashtray or anything else that was handy and flinging it across the room.

This is not unusual for autistic children because they are over-responsive to some stimuli and under-sensitive to other stimuli. Recent research shows that an autistic child may ignore a loud noise but react violently to the sound of crinkling cellophane. This over or under responsiveness to stimuli may be due to the autistic child's inability to integrate incoming sensory input and choose which stimulus to attend to.

Deborah Fein and her colleagues in Boston have an interesting concept of the cause of autism. "In animals autistic-like behavior may result from a lack of input, whereas in autistic children, it may result from failure to attend to input. Because of the very early onset, these children may be deprived of the perceptual experience that normally forms the building blocks of higher percepts, concepts and language." This ties in with earlier studies concerning the inability of autistics to handle simultaneous stimuli and being able to attend to only one aspect of a compound visual or auditory stimulus. Today, even as an adult while waiting in a busy airport, I find I can block out all the outside stimuli and read, but I still find it nearly impossible to screen out the airport background noise and converse on the phone. So it is with autistic children. They have to make a choice of either self-stimulating like spinning, mutilating themselves, or escape into their inner world to screen out outside stimuli. Otherwise, they become overwhelmed with many simultaneous stimuli and react with temper tantrums, screaming, or other unacceptable behavior. Self-stimulating behaviors help calm an over aroused central nervous system. Some researchers believe that autistic children have a hyperactive nervous system, and some children with hyperactive behavior have a slow nervous system. The autistic child self-stimulates to calm himself and the hyperactive child is excessively active because he is trying to stimulate an under aroused nervous system.

Miss Cray, our governess, took advantage of my distress at noise. She used sound as a means of punishment. If I daydreamed, my spoon in mid-air, while eating lunch, Miss Cray would say, "Temple, eat. If you don't finish your soup right now, I'll pop a paper bag at you." She kept a supply of paper sacks on top of the refrigerator so that she could burst them in my face if I misbehaved or drifted away from the world of people. This sensitivity to noise is common among adult autistics. Even today, sudden loud noises such as a car backfiring, will make me jump and a panicky feeling overwhelms me. Loud, high-pitched noises such as a motorcycle's sound, are still painful to me.

But as a child, the "people world" was often too stimulating to my senses. Ordinary days with a change in schedule or unexpected events threw me into a frenzy, but Thanksgiving or Christmas was even worse. At those times our home bulged with relatives. The clamor of many voices, the different smells — perfume, cigars, damp wool caps or gloves — people moving about at different speeds, going in different directions, the constant noise and confusion, the constant touching, were overwhelming. One very, very overweight aunt, who was generous and caring, let me use her professional oil paints. I liked her. Still, when she hugged me, I was totally engulfed and

I panicked. It was like being suffocated by a mountain of marshmallows. I withdrew because her abundant affection overwhelmed my nervous system.

But I survived those first five years — not always with grace, but invariably with gumption. My mother kept a diary and in it she noted:

When bored or tired, Temple spits or takes off her shoes and throws them at something, often giggling while she does this. Sometimes these actions seem beyond her control and other times they are deliberate in order to create a sensation. She becomes less reasonable as the day progresses and her strange behavior appears more impulsive. For instance, she will spit and then get a cloth and wipe it up, as though she knew she shouldn't, but couldn't resist the impulse. Often she will bring a pencil and paper to me and want me to draw a picture. In the morning if I say, 'You draw one for me,' she will oblige. But in the evening this same request is met with anger. She flings the pencil across the room in rage. She picks it up crying, "Bro, bro" (broken). She knows the pencil will break if she throws it, but she cannot resist her angry fling.

Temple seems to be strung on a very fine wire of rationality. If she is crossed, her reactions are bizarre, increasingly so with the degree of fatigue or frustration. Yet, she is aware that her strange behavior perplexes people and so she will feign it simply to amuse herself and create a dramatic situation.

My beautiful child. " . . . when she is good, she is very, very good and when she is

*bad, she is horrid." I must say though, that
even on her worst days, she is intelligent and
exciting. Temple is fun to be with and a dear
companion.*

Mother filled out a Diagnostic Check List for
Behavior-Disturbed Children. Her answers concerning
my behavior show some of the typical, autistic
characteristics. (See Appendix A, page 151.)

CHAPTER TWO

Early School Days

When I was five years old, I went to kindergarten. This was a mixed bag of emotions. Mother told me how much fun school would be, about knowing other children, learning new things. It sounded like fun, but I was fearful. New surroundings upset me and I was not sensitive to social amenities. Fortunately, I didn't realize how different I was. My speech was not like other children's; I missed the subtleties of language; sometimes I escaped into my inner world; and sometimes my behavior was so impulsive and bizarre it startled even me.

The school I attended was a small private school for normal children. Mother had discussed my problems extensively with the teachers. On the first day of school I was kept home so that the teachers could explain to the other children that I was different. The teacher, Mrs. Clark, had short grey hair, and the neck of her dress came almost to her chin. Her face was white like a sheeted ghost, and glasses rested on the tip of her nose. I remember she wore a strong perfume that made me sick to my stomach every time she got too close to me. After drilling us in the different sounds of letters, Mrs. Clark gave each of us workbooks with pictures. On one page there was a box, a suitcase, a bird bath, a chair, a telephone and a bicycle. Mrs. Clark said, "Mark the pictures that began with 'b'."

I marked the suitcase because I thought it was a box. I skipped the picture of the bird and bird bath. They were in the middle of a garden and I thought 'g' was the key sound for them. But I couldn't speak well enough to explain to Mrs. Clark why I had or had not marked certain

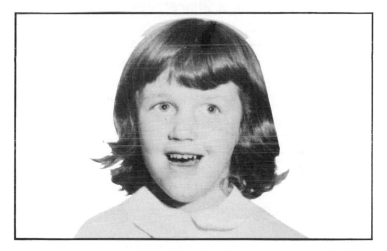

pictures. I understood the concept of the 'b' sound, and I had a logical reason for every mark I made. Frustration raged within me and I wanted to hit or kick to release the feeling. I remember thinking that the bird bath was in the middle of a garden and so obviously, it was related to the 'g' sound. I marked the suitcase with a 'b' because boxes are containers and the suitcase was a box-like container. Even if I could have explained my thinking to Mrs. Clark, she couldn't have accepted such logic—my reasoning didn't fit into the black or white, right or wrong method of teaching.

Another challenge of school was learning rhythm, an impossible task for me. Mrs. Clark would have us sit in a circle and she'd sit at the piano. "Now, children, listen to the beat." She'd play a few bars. "Now, clap your hands in time with the music." I couldn't do it. When the class clapped, my hands were apart.

"Temple. Pay attention."

Mrs. Clark played again. And again I was out of "clap." "Why are you acting this way? You're spoiling it for everyone," she said.

At that moment I didn't want to spoil it, but I couldn't listen to the music and clap my hands rhythmically at the same time.

Mrs. Clark started the song again, but this time, when I was out of clap, she said, "Just fold your hands in your lap, Temple, since you don't want to keep time with the others." Her tone of voice infuriated me.

And then the children laughed. Angry, I jumped up from my chair, knocking it over. Mrs. Clark jumped up, grabbed my shoulder, and led me to the corner of the room where I stood until the clapping exercise was over. Even now, as an adult, when people are clapping in time with the music at a concert, I have to follow the person sitting beside me. I can keep rhythm moderately well by myself, but it is extremely difficult to synchronize my rhythmic motions with other people or with a musical accompaniment.

This is not unusual in autistic children. For them handling two motor tasks at the same time is almost impossible. Research indicates that autistics have a right-left delay in body movements. Getting all the parts to work together is a monumental task.

My inability to handle rhythm was evident also in

school compositions. Here is the poem I wrote for a 5th grade assignment:

The Dark Ages

The Teutrons had a terribul time,
With the terribul Huns.
The huns came in like a shower of spears
And from the fort a hero peers.
When Teutrons gained some power,
Then they drove back terribul Huns.

All this time is the Dark Ages,
But the munks read many books,
And but one munk sit and cooks.
The munks made plans for a new monistary
The wockers built with the greatest of ease,
When one munk sits and eats pease.

The rooms in the monistary are so small,
But the munks are comtible, no matter how tall.
They have their living quarters,
And in the dinning room they eat,
Being humble as a munk should be.
Munks are kind and help the poor.

A munk fond a poor, poor man,
And gave him water in a pan.
He brought him to the monistary,
A fed him lots and lots of food.
The poor man was so very happy,
A soon the poor man became a munk.

The teacher wrote on the composition: "Temple, as history, it's correct — as poetry it has no *rhythm*. With your ability you owe it to yourself to take more care." I did care, but my inability to express my feelings and thoughts rhythmically sabotaged my desires.

In the second grade I began dreaming about a magical device that would provide intense, pleasant pressure stimulation to my body. In my imagination this wonderful machine would not be a substitute for Mother's hugs, but would be available at any time to soothe me.

As an adult, I know now that my childish visions of a magic machine was my search for a means to satisfy my damaged nervous system's craving for tactile stimulation. Since the governess, who lived with us from the time I was three until I was ten years old, never hugged or touched my sister or me, I craved tender touching. I ached to be loved — hugged. At the same time I withdrew from over-touch as from my overweight, overly affectionate, "marshmallow" aunt. Her affection was like being swallowed by a whale. Even being touched by the teacher made me flinch and draw back. Wanting but withdrawing. My brain-damaged nervous system imprisoned me. It was as if a sliding glass door separated me from the world of love and human understanding. There is a balance in teaching the autistic child the joy of touch and panicking the autistic child with the fear of engulfment. At the age of ten I scored a 9 out of a possible 15 on the Ayres checklist for tactile defensiveness. Tactile defensiveness behavior and hypersensitivity are similar. Wool clothing, for instance, is still intolerable for me to wear. I like the pressure of turtle neck shirts. I dislike nightgowns because the feeling of my legs touching each other is unpleasant. Even as an adult, it is difficult for me to sit still for a glaucoma test or to allow a doctor to remove wax from my ear.

Tactile stimulation for me and many autistic children is a no-win situation. Our bodies cry out for human contact but when contact is made, we withdraw in pain and confusion. It wasn't until I was in my mid-twenties that I could shake hands or look directly at someone.

But, as a child, since I had no magical, comfort device, I wrapped myself in a blanket or got under sofa cushions to satisfy my desire for tactile stimulation. At night I tucked in the sheets and blankets tightly and then slid in under them. Sometimes I wore cardboard posters like a sandwich board man because I enjoyed the pressure of the boards against my body.

This need for tactile stimulation is not limited to children with autistic characteristics. Research shows that babies raised in institutions fail to thrive unless they receive cuddling, and premature babies benefit by tactile and kinesthetic stimulation. Even young monkeys, deprived of contact with their mothers, will cling to a terry-clothed paint roller to get "contact comfort."

Some authorities believe that deprivation of tactile stimuli can cause hyperactivity, autistic behavior, violence and aggression. Others feel that even negative body contact is better than none. Some research has been done on the premise that violence may be related to inadequate somatosensory (of the five senses) stimulation. Because of sensory dysfunction, autistic children crave added tactile stimulation. They prefer (proximal) sensory stimulation such as touching, tasting and smelling as opposed to distant (distal) sensory stimulation of hearing or seeing. In the developing nervous system the proximal senses develop first. In birds and mammals the tactile senses develop first. This may explain why a child with a damaged or immature nervous system prefers the proximal senses.

The important thing is getting enough stimulation and it has to be relevant—the child has to know from where the stimulation is coming. In this way the child learns that certain behaviors bring on painful stimulation and other behaviors constitute pleasant stimulation.

Besides negative and positive stimulation, I remember the need to feel I was in control of the amount and type of stimulation I'd tolerate. It was a conflict situation. In order to get over the tactile defensiveness, I needed tactile stimulation but I withdrew. Babies deprived of cuddling avoid being touched when they get older.

When I outgrew wrapping myself in a blanket or crawling under a sofa pillow, I tried to figure out another means for pleasant stimulation. Maybe some sort of machine. Even as a youngster, I liked mechanisms. The first model of the "machine" I dreamed up was an inflatable suit which would apply pressure to my body. I got this idea from plastic inflatable beach toys. In fact, I had many inflatable toys which I sometimes cut up. But even when the toy was cut in pieces, I still liked to play with it. Sometimes I'd cut arm holes in the plastic "remains" so I could wear it like a shirt.

While daydreaming during class in the third grade, I visualized a different type of comfort machine. This design was sort of a coffin-like box. I imagined crawling in the open end. Once inside, I would lay on my back, inflate a plastic lining which would hold me tightly but ever so gently. And most importantly, even in my imagination, I controlled the amount of pressure exerted by the plastic lining.

Another idea I had in grade school was to build a small enclosure about three feet wide and three feet tall—just big enough so I could get into it and close the door. This miniature enclosure would be heated. Warmth along with pressure was important in most of my imaginary designs. Recent research indicate that certain stimuli and stereotyped behavior seem to reduce arousal. Warmth and pressure tend to lessen arousal, especially in a damaged nervous system. Perhaps if I had had a magical comfort machine, I could have used its warmth and pressure instead of throwing a temper tantrum. My imaginary designs were a fixation — an obsession that was refined and improved with each imaginary, magical machine.

Another fixation I had in the fourth grade almost drove my family bonkers. I talked constantly about election posters, buttons, and bumper stickers. I was fixated on the election of our state governor. All I talked about was his election to office. My friend, Eleanor Griffin, and I once spent an entire afternoon removing two election posters from telephone poles so we could tack them up in our bedrooms. Eleanor held my bike steady while I stood teeter-tottering on the bike seat and struggled to remove the tacks holding the election posters.

Constantly asking questions was another of my annoying fixations, and I'd ask the same question and wait with pleasure for the same answer — over and over again. If a particular topic intrigued me, I zeroed in on that subject and talked it into the ground. It was no wonder I was nicknamed "Chatterbox."

Obsessive questioning and perseveration on one subject has been observed in other cases of youngsters who have recovered fully or partially from autism. Even in bed at night I had to talk — tell stories to myself out loud. It wasn't enough to just *think* about a story. It had to be told aloud — otherwise it didn't seem real to me. One of the main characters in my made-up stories was Bisban, an actor from the Our Gang/Little Rascals series. The best thing about my Bisban character was his ability to control things. I wanted to control things and Bisban was my alter-ego. Bisban controlled the blinds, the thermostat, the light in the refrigerator. He could pull strings and make anything happen. But my Bisban did all kinds of naughty things, too, like tying Daddy's shoelaces together or putting salt in the sugar bowl or gluing the toilet lid and seat together. That really made me laugh! Sometimes when I was telling myself Bisban stories out loud, I laughed and laughed and laughed.

By the time I was eleven years old, I had increased my cast of characters, and Alfred Costello was often in my made-up stories. Alfred, a real person, was in my class at school and he teased me all the time. He made fun of the way I talked, tripped me when I walked down the aisle, and called me names like "dummy" or "weirdo." He was the school troublemaker, the class joker, the bane of every teacher. He was the one who put a garter snake in the teacher's grade book, a mouse in the bottom drawer of her desk, and a worm in the apple he gave her. Alfred was a mischievous character in real life and a nasty villain in my made-up stories. In my stories Alfred threw garbage around the school grounds or stuck his tongue out at the teacher. And I laughed as I told the story out loud to myself. And when, in my stories, Alfred got caught, I laughed and laughed and laughed.

Uncontrollable laughter, constant questioning and talking, an obsession with a particular topic (like mine with elections) are common characteristics of autistic-type children. My fixations reduced arousal and calmed me. Too many therapists and psychologically-trained people believe that if the child is allowed to indulge his fixations, irreparable harm will result. I do not think this is true in all cases. Fixations can be guided into something constructive. Taking the fixation away can be unwise. Just as a bad habit is expunged only to be replaced by another bad habit, so it is with a fixation. But making a positive action out of a fixation can be rewarding. A fixation on a particular topic can lead to communication—perhaps isolated communication, but at least a break-through in communication. If properly guided, an autistic child can be motivated by a fixation. A compulsive talking fixation in a child can release some of the pent-up frustration and isolation that an autistic child so often feels.

An autistic child's frustration is all encompassing, touching all phases of learning. I was the last person in my fourth grade class to get the penmanship award. This was a big deal to the children because when the penmanship was good enough, the teacher designated you as "scribe" and you were given a set of colored pencils. I didn't care so much about the "title," but I coveted the colored pencils. I tried very hard and still I was last to qualify. Math was another problem area for me. I couldn't keep up. Just when I would begin to understand a concept, the teacher would introduce a new area of math. Learning math was even more difficult because I had a British teacher, Mr. Brown. He was a very proper Englishman and made the class do the math problems with a fountain pen. We had to rule the plus and minus signs and be ever so neat. It was bad enough trying to understand math but having to be neat besides was impossible. No matter how hard I tried, my papers were splattered with ink. And just as I would begin to understand a math concept, he moved onto the next chapter.

Reading was my best subject. Mother helped me each day after school. Thanks to her, my reading ability was above grade level. She accomplished two things. She improved my reading skills by having me read aloud and sound out the words, and she made me feel grown-up by serving me tea. I realize now that the drink was hot lemon water with a tea flavor, but at the time it was pure, grown-up tea. She helped me educationally and raised my self-esteem.

One subject made school bearable for me and that was art — creating something special out of cardboard or with paints or paste. From the time I was a little girl, I liked to make things. At the time no attention was paid to the wholistic, global artistic side of the brain or the linear, sequential language side of the brain. But obviously, an art-centered curriculum would have encouraged me to learn. In fourth grade Eleanor Griffin and I were the first girls to be allowed to take wood-shop. I loved it and was proud of the model ship and planter I built. Eventually we had to return to the traditional cooking class, and I was a failure again.

I was an absolute terror to the French teacher and was kicked out of her class because I said, *"Mademoselle Jo-Lee, ferme la bouche."* (Miss Julie, shut your mouth.) Since the French teacher was also the sewing teacher, she couldn't understand why I behaved so well in sewing class and not in French class. Simple. In sewing class I was creating something, and I was especially skilled in embroidery.

Studies about delinquency in gifted young people show that they score high in the area of fluid intelligence and nonverbal thinking as opposed to crystalized intelligence, which requires previous training and education. Crystallized intelligence makes use of verbal mediation, sound inference, and sequential steps of logic in problem solving. Crystallized intelligence is rewarded in our educational system in which regurgitation of knowledge is accorded value. As a consequence, many gifted young people who possess fluid intelligence don't fit into the typical educational structure. Another study has shown that some people are gifted in the ability to process large amounts of information and see a pattern where others only see randomness. This unique skill enables them to find the correct answer to a complex problem such as handicapping horse races. This ability is not measurable on the usual I.Q. tests and thus the system incorrectly labels these individuals, and they become outcasts. Often it isn't because the gifted young person wants to be naughty or different, but more often it is because that gifted young person "hears a different drummer."

Creativity—doing something with my hands or imagination—was the beat I heard. For instance, in our fourth grade history class we were studying cavemen and our assignment was to make stone tools such as the cavemen might have had. No modern materials like glue or string were to be used. This was right up my alley. Eleanor Griffin and I spent an afternoon chipping a stone to make a spear and then tying it with vines to a stick. Another class project was a visit to the art museum where we saw mummies in the Egyptian exhibits. I was fascinated, visually stimulated, and recounted all sorts of details to my family about this wonderful excursion. But to read about this or other historical events in the social studies book was boring and I'd sit in a corner and escape to my inner world where I dreamed of my magical box which cradled me like warm, loving arms . . .

My reputation in elementary school was shaded with impulsive, erratic behavior, temper tantrums, and the worst report card possible, but I also was known for unique and creative abilities. When our school had a pet show and everyone was asked to bring a pet, I brought me. Since Mother didn't want me to bring our dog and have him tied up all day at school, I dressed up as a dog. I even had masters—the Reese twin boys. For the entire day I performed like a dog—barking, sitting up, lying down. I was a big hit and was rewarded with a blue ribbon. The next year the class had a toy show and I went as a toy—a rag doll. These original ideas were well received by the school.

My original ideas, good or naughty, were what made Crystal Swift like me. We'd spin around on swings and play word association games. Our laughter over the word "jello" followed by "lime," and then "gravy" was endless. No one else thought it was funny. She could understand my speech with its rounded syllables when others couldn't. When one of the kids asked Crystal why she played with such a nerd as Temple, Crystal said, "I like her because she's not boring."

Eleanor Griffin, who continued to be my friend throughout elementary school, and I used to build tree forts together. Eleanor was well behaved. One day I got mad because someone mimicked my speech and jerky movements in assembly hall, and I threw myself on the floor and kicked everyone who came near me. Eleanor was horrified. Still she remained my friend and defended me against the teasers and taunters. She liked the way I drew horses. When I sang "America, the Beautiful" in front of the entire school, Eleanor clapped the loudest.

In fifth grade I became involved in helping the third grade teacher make costumes for school plays. This was something I enjoyed, and I was extremely good at it. It all relates to making things, being creative and imaginative. Even in the games at school I tried to be creative. We used to play hide and seek. In order to confuse the goalkeeper so I could come in and touch "free," I'd take my coat off and stuff it with leaves and then put it where the goalkeeper would see it. When he went to tag the stuffed coat, I'd run to the goal and win. I always tried to think of new ways of doing things.

I was also quite good at unique and creative ways of being naughty. One time when I was visiting my friend, Sue Hart, we were playing in her hayloft. From the loft we looked down on the garden of Mrs. McDonnell, our fourth grade teacher. Sue said, "Bet you can't throw the red jack ball into Mrs. McDonnell's bird bath."

So I threw the ball from the loft and bounced it out

of the bird bath. For some reason, I don't know why, there were about a hundred big brown empty whiskey bottles up in that hayloft. Sue said, "Why don't you throw a whiskey bottle out?"

So I threw the bottle and it smashed the bird bath. (Today, Sue, the instigator of these monstrous acts, is a high official in the federal government.) We proceeded to throw every one of those whiskey bottles out of the hayloft against the fourth grade teacher's chimney, her sidewalk, her porch, her rose bushes. There was broken glass all over her garden.

The next day in school Mrs. McDonnell told the class about the terrible damage that had been done to her garden. I wasn't about to get caught so at lunch time I sat down next to Mrs. McDonnell in the cafeteria. "Mrs. McDonnell, what a terrible thing to happen to your lovely garden," I said.

"Thank you, Temple, for caring." Mrs. McDonnell smiled warmly at me.

For once, I looked her straight in the eye and told her that I had no idea who had ruined her garden. "But I was at my friend Sue's house," I said, "and we saw Robert Lewis and Burt Jenkins near your house yesterday."

"Thank you for telling me this, Temple. You're a nice little girl to care." Mrs. McDonnell stood up and marched over to the table where Robert and Burt were sitting. I watched as she led them to the principal's office. And I didn't feel bad for getting them in trouble. They *might* have done it *if* they'd thought of it. Besides, it served them right for being so mean and teasing me. As an adult, I know this was a rotten thing to do to those boys. But as an autistic child, unable to fight back physically or verbally, it seemed justified.

Another time we were visiting my cousin, Peter Nash. Peter was always in trouble. One time he burned down a warehouse. This day we were sitting on the front steps of his house. "Dumb neighbors," Peter grumbled. "They told my father I cut across their lawn all the time. Damn tattletales."

I nodded.

"Now, I got to walk all around the block to get to my friend's house." Peter stared at the neighbor's yard. "I'd sure like to fix them."

The idea just jumped out of my mouth. "We could wreck their lawn. You know, throw garbage all over it and then dig it up with one of those metal claws."

Peter sat up straighter. "Yeah. We could." Then he slumped back against the steps again. "But I sure don't want to get blamed."

"Who's to blame?" I asked, giggling. "The dogs did it." We set to work and tore up that lawn like a pack of mongrels and never got caught.

But I did get caught the weekend when I wore tennis shoes to church. Dad yelled at me. I ran out of the church with him right behind me. He finally cornered me between the gas station and a chain link fence. My father had a quick temper. In fact, his side of the family was noted for bad tempers. Recently, research at UCLA found a pattern of inherited traits in some families with autistic children. Like the recessive trait of blue eyes is inherited, so might the autistic characteristics like temper tantrums be passed from generation to generation. To a much lesser (and normal) extent, my father has traits that I have, such as nervousness and a tendency to become totally engrossed in one subject like mutual funds or the details of planning a trip.

As an adult, I've learned to control my temper. My method of control is simple. I never allow my temper to be aroused. I don't argue with people. I just turn and leave a troublesome situation. I don't ever want to unleash my temper. I've seen temper destroy possessions, friendships, families. In junior high school my temper got me into serious trouble.

CHAPTER THREE

New Worries

Near the end of the third grade my parents thought that summer camp might be beneficial for me, and they chose a camp whose staff they felt would be understanding.

Mother asked, "Would you like to go to summer camp, Temple?"

I didn't answer. Part of me wanted to go very much. Many of the kids at my school went to summer camp—but another part of me hesitated. Different people. Different surroundings. Different experiences. Change was not easy for me.

"At camp you'll do crafts, take nature walks. Boat. And swim. Lots of swimming, Temple," Mother continued.

Shortly after school let out, Mother drove me to the camp. It was near the Massachusetts seashore in Cape Cod. All the way to camp I'd talked non-stop with questions about activities, people, and the place.

"Temple, you know as much as I," Mother said and smiled. "Remember the picture in the brochure? There were children swimming and others were in a boat."

"Where will I sleep?"

Mother laughed. "You know, Temple. Remember the picture of the cabins? I told you that you'd be in one of those cabins with seven other children and one grown-up counselor. Remember?"

"Yes. But how will I know which is my cabin?"

"Someone will show you. You're going to have a wonderful summer with new friends and new adventures."

When Mother drove into the dusty parking lot, a young woman hurried to meet us. I wished I could hide. The cabins looked bigger than in the brochure picture and there were lots of people running around, yelling and laughing.

"Welcome to Camp Swanee." The woman opened the door on my side of the car. "You're Temple Grandin, aren't you? I'm Nan Armen, the counselor in your cabin."

I looked at the floorboard. I didn't move.

"Get out, Temple, and speak to Nan." Mother stood beside the young woman.

I felt hot on the outside but inside I was ice. Slowly I stepped out of the car. In a few minutes Nan was showing me my cabin, my bunk, the footlocker for my clothes. When it came time for Mother to leave, I could barely say goodbye I was so busy getting on my suit for swimming.

That first swim set the stage for a new fixation for me and new worries for my parents. I was sitting on my towel to take off my tennis shoes. A boy, maybe eleven or twelve years old, said to his friend. "Don't bother looking at the newcomer. No boobs at all."

"Boobs?" I repeated and the boys laughed.

The rest of the afternoon "boobs" was my favorite word. It was a new word. I loved the feel of it in my mouth. In my perseverative manner I said it over and over. Everytime I said it, the boys laughed. Later, in the cabin, I said the word. Nan frowned. "Temple, we don't use that word in mixed company." She explained what "boobs" were. But it was too late—the word was in my head and continued to slide off my tongue regularly.

One of the girls from my cabin walked with me to the mess hall for dinner that night. She whispered that girls have boobs so that they can feed their babies.

"Don't boys want to feed babies?" I asked.

With pursed lips, the girl said, "A boy has something else. Something that *makes* babies."

"I've never seen it. Where do they keep it?"

"In their pants, dummy!" She laughed. "If you're so interested, why don't you ask one of the boys to see his 'peter?' "

The next day at swimming I did. The boy's eyes widened; his mouth dropped down; he stammered, "What?"

I repeated my request.

"You crazy or something?" He walked away. A few

minutes later I saw him talking with his friend. They pointed at me and laughed.

The rest of the week passed happily. I swam and boated and made a shell necklace during craft time. The boys teased me, but not meanly. They'd say things I didn't understand like "You're ripe," and I'd answer, "Yes, I'm ripe. Ripe. Ripe." And they'd laugh. But when I repeated some of these things to Mrs. Northrop, the camp director, or to Nan, my cabin counselor, or to Lynda, the craft instructor, they didn't laugh, but turned away or looked down at their feet. This didn't stop me. I was obsessed with my new vocabulary.

At the end of the first week I became ill. I woke up on Friday with a fever and chills, and it hurt to urinate. Nan took me to the infirmary where the nurse put me to bed. After the camp doctor had made his diagnosis, he prescribed gentian violet for my urinary infection. All that week I was kept in bed. Twice a day the nurse painted my genitals with the purple medicine. Then she'd stick a cotton swab up my vagina which hurt so much I cried. Sometimes she'd take a sharp instrument like the dentist uses and probe my genital area. She gave me pills that made me sleepy. A week later, when Mother came to get me, I couldn't remember how long I'd been in the infirmary.

After I had recovered at home from my infection, Mother and Dad visited Dr. Stein, a child psychiatrist, recommended by the pediatrician who had cared for me since infancy. Mother wrote after their consultation:

Dear. Dr. Stein:

I came home from our interview slightly disturbed, not by your intimations as to the cause of Temple's maladjustments, but by the tangent my husband got off on at the end of our meeting. I

47

*think my husband longs for vindication and both
Dr. Pelham (Temple's pediatrician) and Mrs. Dee
(Temple's third grade teacher) feel he is justified.
The point is not whether the child has this habit
or that, but rather the way in which the child per-
forms and acts. The same characteristics turn up
to some degree in all children, but it is the compulsive quality of her behavior that is the problem.
It has also been the point of greatest improvement. When Temple is in secure surroundings
where she feels love above all, and appreciation,
her compulsive behavior dwindles. Her voice loses
its curious stress and she is in control of herself.
At home there is no problem. In the neighborhood
with a few close friends she manages better all the
time. She and two other little girls have been great
pals. She appreciates them and they her. They play
together as Temple could never have played last
summer and last summer these two little girls did
not like her at all. Their whole relationship has
been that of three normal, happy, little girls. At
school her behavior improves. Difficulties occur
when she is tired or when she returns to school
after vacation and has to adjust again. Large,
noisy groups confuse her. With work she wastes a
lot of energy complaining, flinging herself around,
but finally buckles down to work. She wants
someone near her in whom she has confidence.
Her improvement is tied in, I'm sure, with appreciation and love. Until she is secure in her surroundings, knows the boundaries and feels accepted and actively appreciated, her behavior is erratic.*

*In any therapy with Temple (and let us consider
that your premise of psychic injury is correct) the*

most important point seems to be love. As if to make up for love she could not give or receive in her early years, she can only operate successfully now when she feels love. Those who teach her genuinely enjoy her company and they get the best response. Her peers at school have learned to accept her eccentricities. She provides information and enrichment. I heard one little girl say, "I like Temple because she has lots of ideas and makes things." At the end of a particularly successful day when Temple came home full of talk about "my friends," she went to her room and tidied like mad—because she was happy and loved—and therefore wanted to be good and knew that I would be pleased if she picked up the room. She will say, "I love you, Mummie," and this is because she is feeling happy. The two are synonymous.

Valley Country Day school has done extremely well in helping Temple live with her nervous disposition and in developing her talents. Her teacher, Mrs. Dee, feels Temple needs familiar surroundings and that those handling her should deal firmly with her eccentricities rather than being shocked by them. Temple needs to learn the boundaries of a new situation. Her sportsmanship is poor and she does badly in organized competitive games. She can compete individually. She is talented artistically and proud of her art work and sewing. Mrs. Dee feels most of all that Temple needs responsive affection and there must always be a bond between her and the adult.

Most of us instinctively pattern our lives to please those around us and by this acquire a sense of suitability. Temple either lacks this desire to conform or her nervous impulse is too great for her to overcome. Perhaps a little of each.

There is nothing morbid or difficult for us in caring for Temple. And I don't feel sorry for us. It is frequently exciting and not uninspiring for it seems to bring out the best in people. Each person who has dealt with Temple has given generously of themselves and she has responded. I am deeply touched by their concern and love. I suppose that is why I am so disappointed by the camp episode. They are the first people to fail. Largely because of an archaic view about sex, I think they panicked.

Also, Mrs. Dee, Temple's third grade teacher, had told Mrs. Northrup, the camp director, that an experienced counselor should be in Temple's cabin. Although Nan was young, pretty, and pleasant, she did not give the impression of vast experience. So Mrs. Northrup, feeling guilty, took the easy way out and blamed Temple. Her accusations are pretty strong. Saying that she and her staff were older and wiser than we, she claimed Temple was sexually advanced, over-sexed and unnaturally obsessed with sex. A good many of these accusations were delivered over the telephone in a hushed but excited voice. Mrs. Northrup said, "I heard one young boy say to another, 'She made a pass at me,' whatever that means." Then realizing she sounded rather foolish, she added, "I know this is an expression young people use, but I do not know exactly what it means."

Dr. Stein, in my opinion, the main problem was Temple's urinary infection which itched and hurt and Temple kept touching herself. After the camp doctor treated her with gentian violet, the nurse

remarked, *"You see, the child has masturbated."*
(The Scarlet Letter *syndrome!) The second problem was the camp personnel's lack of insight.
Temple always tries people out almost as if to find
the boundaries of her behavior. An experienced
counselor would have realized this. But no one at
this camp stopped Temple's questions about
babies, sexual differences, taboo words, but rather
saved up all of the incidents and then compared
notes. Temple did say, "Mrs. Northrup didn't
want me to use some words so I didn't to her."*

*I didn't sense any enjoyment of Temple from
anyone in the camp. They couldn't wait to get her
out. Not until Temple was in the car ready to
leave, did the nurse allow herself to say with
transparent heartiness, "Just wait until you see the
wonderful things Temple made in the infirmary.
She's quite a little artist." I longed to snort. The
child had been kept so heavily sedated that she
could not have drawn a straight line. I'm not trying to make out a case for Temple, but to indicate
that perhaps her compulsive behavior took a sexual turn due to the nature of her infection—not
that she is a pervert about to go into puberty (the
camp's interpretation). It enrages me that the child
was sedated and the camp did not admit it. The
odd thing about these people, the Northrups, is
that they gave every impression of warmth, acceptance and competence. Perhaps, if her sin had
been anything but sexual, they could have dealt
admirably. They are the first people we have run
into who did not try to reach Temple. The saddest
part is that Temple loved the camp and remembers
all its details with affection.
Often when life gets difficult for Temple, she*

gains an oddly mature insight about herself. The first time she had a swimming lesson, she couldn't manage and kicked and thrashed around. The swimming instructor, a good-natured boy, was patient and fun, but he was firm with her. After it was over, Temple asked me why she had so much trouble learning to run herself. After a bit of introspection she took a stride forward. Another time, she remarked that it was difficult, this learning to live and took another stride forward. She would not learn to ride a bicycle, but after being left out, to her bitter disappointment, she got to work and learned rapidly. Since coming home from camp, she has seemed older. I know that she has turned it over considerably in her mind. Her little flashes of insight may be the clue to help her on her way.

I'm glad this meeting with you has come about, not as a desperate last resort, but to further aid Temple's successful maturity. If she is an emotional cripple, at least she does not know it. She is a happy child.

Please do not be alarmed at breaking a dramatic diagnosis to us. One does not stop loving one's child because some psychic wound has been interpreted. The child is still the same child, the family the same family and quite possibly the treatment the same treatment. One great advantage of bringing up children is the process is constant and daily—not a great unwieldy problem to be solved in three days.

Unless you feel Temple will fall apart hopelessly in adolescence, I do not see that the picture has changed. If you feel that psychiatry is in order, naturally we will be most anxious to follow your advice. I am interested and curious to know why Dr. Cruthers and Dr. Meyes, both of whom I admire tremendously, recommended normal therapy when Temple was three years old, rather than abnormal. I would like to hear your opinion. We have been enormously helped by the professional thought and advice we've been given. We owe a great debt to the St. Luke's Hospital. It is with gratitude and confidence that we return for further consultation.

Sincerely,
Mrs. Grandin

After further consultation, my parents took me to the psychiatrist once a week. Dr. Stein was a German, schooled in Freudian theory. Supposedly, he would probe my innermost subconscious secrets and discover what made me act weird. (Psychological theory in 1956 theorized that autism was caused by a psychic injury. Modern knowledge in the neurosciences indicates that this is rubbish. Autism is caused by damage to the central nervous system. It is a physiological problem.)

To me, Dr. Stein looked like one of the men on the Smith Bros. Cough Drops package. He was the nice guy I talked to and played games with. He kept M & M's in a candy dish on his desk for me to enjoy. Ferreting out the roots of my mythical psychic injury was impossible, but Dr. Stein was helpful because he advised Mother on how to work with me. Mother had taught me to read; she defended me when I got into trouble at school; her good instincts worked better than hours of expensive therapy.

Since I knew the psychiatrist talked to Mother privately, I did not tell him certain things.

I was not at all sensitive to the relationships of people around me. When my mother and father began to have marital problems, my sister Jean would say, "Do you think Mother and Dad will get divorced?" "Of course not," I would reply stoutly. Since they did not yell at one another in my presence, I was unable to sense the more subtle signs of friction between them. I got along well with Jean, who was a year and a half younger than I. My other brother and sister were six and eight years younger than I, so Jean and I grew up together while the two younger siblings were companions.

Another thing I never told the psychiatrist was my desire to build a device that would provide contact comfort. Even I sensed that such an idea would go under the "weird" column on my chart. But instead of being drowned in a tidal wave of uncontrolled stimuli when my overweight aunt hugged me, if I had had a comfort device, perhaps the silly, repetitive sex talk which got me into so much trouble wouldn't have occurred. The advantage of a comfort device would be that I could control the amount of stimuli. I could satisfy my craving for contact comfort without flooding my senses with massive amounts of input my nervous system couldn't tolerate.

One study indicates excessive masturbation in children stops when they receive more affection and hugging from parents. The comfort device that I had in mind would not be a substitute for affection from Mother but it would help my immature and damaged nervous system to learn how to tolerate affection from other people who loved me like my father and my aunt.

Dr. Stein asked me lots of questions about love and who loved me and whom did I love. "How about your friends at school? Did you get along well?" Dr. Stein asked.

"I guess. They tease me a lot though." I helped myself to a fistful of M & M's.

"What do you do?"

"Hit 'em. Sometimes." I put my head back and dropped M & M's in my mouth one by one.

"Temple! Pay attention. I asked you about your father. Go on. What about him? Do you get along?" Dr. Stein's hand made a rolling motion in the air.

No way was I going to tell him about Dad's quick temper. I helped myself to another handful of M & M's and looked up at Dr. Stein. "Sure, Dad gets mad sometimes — just like you or me — but we have lots of fun. Sometimes I help him in the garden. We plant bulbs and weed and trim the roses on the lattice. What I really like doing though is helping him on the boat. I polish the brass fittings. Dad says I'm the best polisher in the whole world." That was true and it was also true that Dad was at his best (as was I) when he was doing physical work.

Dr. Stein nodded and noted something on my chart. For the next two years I visited Dr. Stein regularly and kept the M & M candy company in business.

At the end of fifth grade Mother wrote Dr. Stein again:

Dear Dr. Stein,

I feel it's time for another check with you. Though progress seems good, there are various points I would like to go over with you.

First, at home Temple does better all the time. She is loving, obedient, much neater and genuinely helpful. I wish the outside world saw more of this. She is much more independent in a most healthy and outgoing way.

Secondly, her school work is adequate scholastically, but only under duress. She hates French and frankly has been a terror to the French teacher. She does homework with great reluctance, though there is nothing slow about her mental

*processes when she chooses to use them. I know
this because at the suggestion of her teacher, I
help her nightly with her homework. She has been
making definite progress all year, particularly since
the school has been sending home weekly reports.
This is something I asked for specifically and it
has helped to keep Temple's mind on her school
work. Here is the current scholastic problem. Will
Temple be able to go on from Valley Country Day
to a regular school? Will she be able to keep up
scholastically? Can she manage herself socially?*

*Mr. Johnson, her teacher, feels there is no
reason why not, provided her history is fully
understood and she is in sympathetic hands. The
danger is that realizing her steady advancement,
we will be too eager and optimistic about her
future. It is hard when one is so close to Temple
to come to a calculated and dispassionate conclusion. We need your help.*

*I have a frightening feeling that I have been too
much of a rudder for Temple and I feel she must
build her own rudder. We have this year and next
to prepare her — either to cope with life on her
own in a new school or to be prepared for a different life away from her friends. This must be apparent to her as well as to us if she is to stay on
an even keel. I have tried to show her that she will
go on to another school on her own record. I
don't care where she goes to school, but the choice
will depend on her work — that you, the family,
her teacher can only help, encourage and advise
her — that in the end she makes her own life. The
final choice lies with her. This is a difficult realiza-
tion for a ten-year-old. No matter how much your
family loves you — that is, really loves you — they*

cannot run interference for you.

I have a feeling that I tend to do a snow job on everyone connected with Temple, thereby putting them in a favorable frame of mind to help her. But time is running out and I won't be able to do this much longer. How can I help her? How much pressure can I put on her? I am always surprised how she can turn off bad behavior if she chooses. Right now, she is trying very hard to control herself. How much pressure and discipline can she take from me or the school? Am I helping her or building up horrible emotional blocks for her?

It has always been my premise that discipline from family or a well-loved school person is easier than discipline from strangers. Perhaps you can evaluate the situation.

Sometimes Temple leaves the house because she says I make her life unbearable and yet she counts on that home discipline to guide her. I'm told that she is very responsible too when away from home. There are two families in particular who are fond of her and welcome her at all times.

One point particularly bothers me still and that is the sex business. Mr. Johnson, her teacher, says that there is bathroom chatter and panty talk. I suggested to Temple that this kind of conversation was babyish and embarrassing to others. To my surprise, she denied being an instigator of this sex talk and said that the boys "sicced" her into it. How do I help this situation without disturbing her? We are perplexed and need your help.

But you know, Dr. Stein, there is so much good, so much desire to do well, so much maturity combined with babyishness—all mixed together—that if we can help her understand

herself, she has the makings of a fine person. I
suppose this could be said of any child, but this is
our child. If there are means to be used, let us use
them — and not hold back or delude ourselves.
Temple has tried so hard this year. She deserves
the very best help we all can give her. I look for-
ward to hearing from you.

> *Sincerely,*
> *Mrs. Grandin*

CHAPTER FOUR

Forgettable Days at Junior High

O dell Shepard said, "Quite literally, a man's memory is what he forgets with." My junior high period fits this quotation. Perhaps because this time in my life was most unhappy, I recall only fragments. When I open the door to my memories a crack, I am bombarded with negative impressions. A sense of isolation envelops me. My mouth becomes dry and I can feel myself wanting to escape into my inner world where I'm not overwhelmed with remembrances of noisy hallways jammed with students nor feel cruel peer rejection and teachers' negative attitudes. Typical of young people with autism, I didn't bear change with grace.

After graduating from the Valley County Day School, I entered seventh grade at the Cherry Hill Girls School in Norwich, Connecticut. This was a large private day school made up of upper middle-class girls. It was different from the small elementary school I'd attended with only thirteen students in the class and a single teacher teaching all the subjects. Also, the elementary school had worked closely with my parents.

Entering Cherry Hill Girls School with thirty to forty students in a class and a different teacher for each subject, was a confusing, traumatic experience. I was lost—overwhelmed by the jostling, noisy crowd, and unable to do well in subjects such as math and French because these subjects are not learned visually. They were abstractions and concepts—not precisely represented in terms of objects or figures. The only thing I remember from math class was a hands-on demonstration on the meaning of "pi"—the formula for finding the area of a circle. I remember that the teacher took a cardboard circle and wrapped a string around the circumference and showed the class it equaled three diameters with a little left over which worked out to 3.14. This was real to me. I saw it and understood it. Biology was another class I did well in and again it was visual learning rather than sequential learning. As in elementary school, I did well in creative classes such as jewelry making. We worked with real silver and I was successful in designing unique jewelry. But, again, as in elementary school, when I didn't understand the subject, I became bored and when I became bored, I was naughty. When I think about it now, I realize part of my mischief was the result of boredom but part of it was the thrill of wondering what would happen—the reaction of my peers—and if I'd be caught. A good example of this was gym class, where I'd wait until the other girls had gone into gym and then hide their classroom clothes. When gym was over, I laughed and laughed inside myself as I watched them run around trying to find their clothes. Often they had to wear their gym clothes to the next class. I always hid mine, too, so I wouldn't be a suspect.

Another trick that tickled me was tying the blind cords

to students' desks so that when they opened the desk, the blinds fell down, causing great commotion in class. Jokes like this amused me and relieved the classroom boredom.

Of course, the school contacted Mother about my low grades and my mischief. Mother called Dr. Stein, my psychiatrist, about her concerns. He was a friend of the principal of Cherry Hills Girls School. Dr. Stein wrote:

Dear Jim:

Mrs. Grandin called me last night because she was concerned there might be some misunderstanding among the faculty of your school regarding her daughter, Temple.

I have known the Grandins since July, 1956 but have had treatment contact with Temple mostly from December, 1958 to June, 1959. Temple is one of these unusual children who had a very disturbed early childhood and was at the time, unfortunately, wrongly labeled as having brain damage. Very careful psychological tests done in 1956 and again in 1959, as well as my long-term observation of this child completely contradict this finding. As you know, psychological tests tend to pick up organic disturbances. In 1956 she obtained a full scale I.Q. of 120; in 1959, a full scale I.Q. of 137. She does not function quite up to this very superior level.

Let me express my opinion through the summary given by the psychologists: "In summary then, Temple is a child of extremely high intelligence, whose problems are such that she cannot free her affect at this time and thereby make creative use of this intelligence. On the less positive side, one sees an openess that is a bit much, a level of reality testing that is poor under severe stress, and an impulsive quality that should not be present in an eleven-year-old. On the positive side, one sees no really bizzare material; one sees the working of intellectual controls, a functioning intelligence, and an ability to deal with situations as they come, even though her controls require much of her energy. Temple is not now psychotic, or close to it. One could call her a neurotic child—she has a well formed personality organization, and the controls to maintain this organization except in cases of severe stress. She is still very much in the process of developing the healthier aspects of her personality, and the fluctuations one sees appear to be part of this growth process. She has come an amazing distance since last seen.

I think Temple is a child of enormous potential, unusually imaginative, although some of her oddities may tend to make her a bit conspicuous. Of course, she is now going to go into adolescence and she has left a school which knew her at her worst, was most supportive, and was also pleased with her progress.

Please let me know if there is anything that I can clarify or any way that I can be of assistance to you and your staff. I am sorry we have seen so little of each other in the past two years.

Dr. Stein was right. I was making some progress. For the most part I was trying to blend in—not cause waves—and for a good reason. I had been elected to the assembly committee, which was a big honor. Once a week when the students lined up for assembly, I was the "policeman." If anyone talked or acted up in line I gave her demerits. Because I wanted to be on the assembly committee and I enjoyed the recognition, I cleaned up my act as far as hiding gym clothes and other pranks.

There were other things that marked my progress. I liked watching "Twilight Zone" on television, I enjoyed reading science fiction, and I was intrigued with designing model airplanes. I tried weird new designs to see if I could make them fly. Flying objects was not a new fixation with me. When I was a little kid, I had designed a paper kite to fly behind my tricycle. I found that by making the wings of the kite flat and bending a little flap up on the end of the wings, I got high performance with slightly less stability, but it would fly at a very steep angle. Years later I saw an advertisement in the *Wall Street Journal* that advertised a new corporate jet with little winglets on the end of the wing — just like those I'd put on my paper kite years before. This interest in engineering undoubtedly can be attributed to my engineer grandfather. He and an associate patented the most important component of the automatic pilot. It's called a flux valve and it senses the motion of the plane's wings through the earth's magnetic field. This major invention is still used today on all commercial jets. Grandfather was patient with me and always had time to answer my questions. "Why is the sky blue?" or "What makes the tides go in and out?" I'd ask and he would give me a scientific answer in understandable terms.

But in spite of creative talents, I lacked the ability of getting along with people. As a rule, they didn't warm to my erratic behavior, my stressed way of talking, my bizarre ideas, my jokes and tricks. And my grades overall were deplorable.

But it wasn't the jokes and tricks nor poor grades nor being different that finally got me expelled from Cherry Hills Girls School after two-and-a-half years. It was temper tantrums. Kids teased me and I reacted by smacking them. I'd been warned that such conduct was not acceptable. Still, when Mary Lurie, a girl in my grade, passed me in the hallway on the way to music class, she turned and looked at me. Lifting her nose in the air and curling her lips in a sneer, she spat, "Retard! You're nothing but a retard!"

Anger, hot and quick, ripped through me. I was carrying my history book. Without hesitation I threw my arm back and then forward. My history book zoomed through the air like a guided missile and hit Mary in the eye. She screamed and I walked away, not even bothering to pick up my history book.

That night at home the phone rang and I answered. It was Mr. Harlow, the principal of Cherry Hill Girls School. He didn't even ask to speak to one of my parents. He just said, "Don't bother coming back to school. You are incorrigible. Mrs. Lurie is very upset. You could have blinded Mary and all because of your nasty, uncontrollable temper."

I hung up the phone. Anger and frustration surged through me and I trembled, sick at my stomach. Mr. Harlow hadn't even asked to hear my side of it. He just assumed that since I was "different" I was entirely to blame.

"Who's on the phone, Temple?" Mother called out. "Is it for me?"

"No." I took a deep breath and went into the living room where Mother was reading to my younger sisters and brother. Dad was reading the evening newspaper.

"Well, who was it?" Dad rattled his newspaper.

"Mr. Harlow, the school principal," and I told my parents what he had said.

"Expelled! Oh, Temple!" Mother laid down the book and hurried to me. "What happened?"

I explained and she listened carefully. As usual, she stood up for me. After the younger children had been put

64

to bed and Dad had gone for a walk, we made plans.

In the next few weeks we covered the area looking at different schools. I finally ended up going to a school with which Mother had had considerable contact the previous year. She had been writing scripts for television documentaries and had done one on retarded children. Her script won the Ohio State Award for the best documentary. The other documentary was for PBS and concerned emotionally disturbed children. Much of her research had been centered in the Mountain Country School in Vermont. We toured this school and decided it was the right place for me. Again, it was a small school like Valley Country Day School, the elementary school I had attended before junior high. Mountain Country School had only thirty-two students when I enrolled so that there was a lot of individual attention. I was known as Temple, an individual—not some girl who was different from the many other students at Cherry Hill Girls School. Being in a smaller school with individual attention made it much easier for me to deal with my problems.

But always in the attic of my mind I dreamed of a magical machine that would soothe me and make me less different.

CHAPTER FIVE

Boarding School

In January 1960, Mother drove me to my new school. I stared out the car window at the deep drifts of snow along the highway. One moment I felt as cold with fear and apprehension as the snow and the next moment I fired questions at Mother. "Will I have my own room? You said there were farm animals. Are there horses? Will I get to ride? How much farther? What if I don't like it? Will there be mean boys there?"

Mother laughed, then said, "One question at a time, Temple. The Mountain Country School was started for gifted children like you. Their aim is to help these children reach their highest potential. To be equipped both emotionally and mentally to proceed to top-level schools. And in their eleven years they have been very successful."

"Successful. Successful. I'm going to be successful," I repeated.

"And, Temple, you'll meet new friends."

"And horses."

"Yes, horses and other farm animals. The school offers arts and crafts, and there will be camping and canoe trips. Music, 4-H programs, theater, ballet, bowling, fishing, swimming, skiing, skating. Oh, Temple, I think you're going to really like this school. It seems to have everything."

I leaned my head against the cold pane. Visions of *me* fishing or camping or riding a horse almost filled my head. But one thought wormed its way out of the corner of my mind. "How about math and French? Does the school have those classes?" I asked. I didn't see how I possibly could fit either math or French into a busy schedule of arts and crafts and all the other activities.

"Yes, Temple. The Mountain Country School has French and math and other academic classes, too. This is a place to learn and also a place to have fun and make friends."

Mother steered the car around the sharp mountain curve, and there before us, nestled in among the pine and maple trees, were several large buildings, a barn, and the traditional New England stone walls.

"I see horses!" I shouted, bouncing up and down on the seat.

Mother turned off at the sign, "Mountain Country School, Student Population — 32, Elevation — 1000 feet." She had no sooner parked in front of the largest building when a man hurried down the steps and across the lot to our car. "Welcome, Mrs. Grandin. Welcome. I'm Charles Peters, director of Mountain Country School." He smiled at me. "And you are Temple?" Opening the door, he helped Mother out.

I nodded.

"Come with me. I'll give you a tour and explain some of our plans for you. I think you're going to like it here,

Temple. We have 1900 acres of meadows, lakes, streams, and mountains. Plenty of room to grow in."

For the next hour he guided Mother and me around the grounds, showing us not only the classrooms, theater, and library but also the dairy, the horse stables, and sheep pens. "Young people who are interested in farm animals are allowed to work in the dairy or stables and help care for the animals," Mr. Peters said. "Let's head for my office now, and I'll explain the living arrangements, our academic hopes, and some of our goals for each student."

Leaning back in his office chair, Mr. Peters began. "Here at Mountain Country School we believe in controls because they provide structure for self-discipline and self-reliance — necessary ingredients in adult life. We encourage students to participate in our community life. Such participation teaches individual and group responsibilities; it is a learning experience in handling frustrations; and, most important of all, it shows the individual that he must accept the consequences of his own acts. We're in the business of showing young people the disciplined as well as the creative way of solving problems in their lives."

He pointed out that there were four essential areas for both the school and the individual: an understanding of an individual's personal problems and what to do to correct them; mastery of study skills; developing the social skills essential to everyday association; and the competition of everyday living either in or out of school. The basic philosophy of the school rested upon the principle of permitting students an opportunity to achieve what they could in specific areas, while at the same time both academic and personal allowances were made for areas of emotional handicaps. Direct therapy was offered to students needing more than a therapeutic environment. This involved individual counseling by professional staff to help the student resolve problems of control, limit-setting, and motivation.

"Well, Temple, before we admit you, we want to know how *you* feel about this school. Do you think you'll like being a part of our community?"

His question startled me and my answer was a stressed "Yesss."

"You'll live in one of the family units. And you'll have responsibilities and duties—and fun." He stood up and put out his hand. I pretended I didn't see it. "Glad you're going to be with us, Temple."

Mother walked with me to my "new" family unit. We met the house mother and she showed us to my room.

"Temple, I know you're going to like this school and do very well." Mother, ready to leave, stood at the door. "I guess I'd better be on my way."

I didn't look at her. I put my panties and socks in the top drawer of the dresser.

"The house will seem awfully quiet without you, dear."

I studied the rough ribbing on my knee-high socks and ran my finger across the ridges—over and over. The unevenness of the knitted sock felt good on my finger.

"I'll miss you, Temple." She walked quickly to my side and kissed my cheek. I ached to be enfolded in her arms, but how could she know? I stood rigid as a pole trapped by the approach/avoidance syndrome of autism. I drew back from her kiss, not able to endure tactile stimulation—not even loving, tactile stimulation.

Sitting on the end of the bed, I looked around the room. It had everything I would need—dresser, desk, chair, lamp, and bed. I took the Mountain Country School's brochure from my purse and reread it. With promises of love and understanding, integrated with instruction, religion, recreation, crafts, clinical and psychiatric therapy, the Mountain Country School offered me, an autistic child with frequent, uncontrollable temper tantrums, a chance to learn academically and emotionally.

And learn I did—quickly.

That evening I stood in line with other boarders waiting for the dinner bell. Although there was a lot of talking and laughing all around me, no one said anything to me. Suddenly, a girl a little older than I cut into the line ahead of me.

"Hey, no cuts," I said, stepping in front of her. I heard her sharp intake of breath.

"Bug off, nerd," she said and shoved me.

Impulsively I whirled around and smacked her. She yelled, and suddenly the talking and laughing around me stopped. The dead silence of the room chilled me. An older woman stepped out from the crowd of kids and walked toward me. I wanted to run, hide, scream. Looking very kindly, she walked toward me. When she was at my side, she said, "You're Temple Grandin, aren't you?"

I nodded.

"We need to talk." She took my arm and started to lead me away. Ordinarily I would have balked and jerked away. But there was something about the feel of her silk sleeve blouse against my arm—the steady non-threatening pressure of her arm inside the smooth, soft, slick fabric looped through mine. "Phoebe," she said to the girl who had cut in front of me, "please, save a place at your table for Temple and me."

She took me across the room to a sitting area in the corner. "I'm Miss Downey. Tell me what happened, Temple."

For a moment I was stunned. I wasn't used to being asked my side of an argument or fight. Without looking at Miss Downey, I recounted Phoebe's cutting in line ahead of me.

"That's what I saw, Temple. No one likes to be cut ahead of. But," and Miss Downey reached over and tilted my chin up so that I had to look at her, "hitting is not the way to handle a disagreement." She talked about getting along with people and learning to control my temper. "The Mountain Country School will not tolerate any form of physical abuse. Do you know what I mean?"

"I'm not supposed to smack anyone." I mumbled, again looking down.

"Right. Now let's join the others for dinner. I will talk with Phoebe later about cutting in."

From then on Phoebe didn't cut in on me or anyone else as far as I know, but I still reacted to any problem with a flare of temper and a forceful smack at my tormentor. During my first six months at Mountain Country School I solved any disagreement with fists. Miss Downey was patient and tried to reason with me, but when I smacked a classmate for laughing at me when I tripped over a croquet wire, Miss Downey took away the privilege I lived for — riding horses — for a whole week. I was confined to the dorm except for classes and meals. Words hadn't curbed my fighting spirit nor threats, but not being able to ride horses for seven days smartened me up in a hurry. I still did naughty things in the boring classrooms, but I no longer used my fists to settle a disagreement.

Although my behavior as far as physical fights improved, my fixations worsened. For several years my obsessions, such as election posters, constant questions and endless chatter, had diminished. But with the change in environment, I reacted with nerve attacks. Like most autistic children, I needed to preserve sameness in my environment and the change from home to a rooming and boarding school disturbed me. Like most autistics I wanted everything the same. I even wore the same jacket and dressed in the same kind of clothes day in and day out. And when the housemother wanted me to move to a bigger and better room, I panicked and refused. But one factor I couldn't keep the same was my physical maturing. Hormonal changes experienced at puberty further contributed to my nerve attacks. With the onset of menstruation, the panic attacks increased in intensity. Driven frantically by this changing force, I felt like a windmill in a tornado. Fantasies blew through my mind; my impulsive behavior became more pronounced; I had even more difficulty getting along with the other students. Scholastically disinterested, I was at the bottom of the class in all subjects except biology.

These nerve attacks, complete with pounding heart, dry mouth, sweaty palms, and twitching legs, had the symptoms of "stage fright," but were actually more like hypersensitivity than anxiety. Perhaps this accounts for the fact that Librium and Valium did not provide relief to my trembling body. The panic would worsen as the day progressed and the afternoon hours from two to four in the afternoon were the worst. By nine or ten o'clock at night the anxiety subsided.

Thinking back on this time of my life, I realize that the anxiety I experienced was cyclical. During menstruation, the anxiety lessened. But during the late fall, when the days became shorter, my anxiety attacks worsened. Research indicates that the length of daylight can influence depression. Artificial lengthening of the day with special full spectrum lights can alleviate depression in some people. Also, the anxiety attacks subsided when I was sick and had a fever. (Parents of autistic children have reported that their child's behavior improved during a fever.)

Various stimuli, insignificant to most people, created a full blown stress reaction in me. When the telephone rang or when I checked the mail, I'd have a "stage fright" nerve attack. What if I didn't get any mail—or what if I did—and it was something bad? The ring of the telephone set off the same reaction—panic. Going bowling in the evening made me nervous and I dreaded the school trips. I was afraid I'd be seized by a panic attack in a public place and wouldn't be able to stand it.

An interesting fact about the nerve attacks is that reactions to certain stimuli can become sensitized in a young child and the full reaction does not occur until after puberty. In my case, from ages seven to sixteen I had recurring bouts of pinworms. The itching from the worms annoyed me as a young child, and my parents failed to treat them until they were well established. Prior to puberty the itching was merely irritating, but after puberty the itching triggered a stress reaction with all the physiological symptoms of rapid heart beat, sweating, and anxiety. An ordinary itch, insignificant to most people, created the same reaction in me as being chased by a mugger. Recent research indicates that female hormones can change the sensitivity of the nervous system. This may account for my stressed reaction to the itching caused by the pinworms.

Also, according to recent research, rats which had been handled early in their lives had less stereotyped behavior in response to amphetamine injections (a drug that stimulates the central nervous system) than those that were not handled. Perhaps if I had received more tactile and deep pressure stimulation as a child, my hypersensitivity would have been reduced at puberty.

Other studies suggest that there may be a deficit in the regulation of noradrenergic activity. Noradrenalin is an adrenalin-like substance which stimulates nerve impulses and increases arousal in the brain. The noradrenergic system may alternate between too much or too little activity. According to an article in the *Journal of Autism*

and Developmental Disorders by G.L. Young and colleagues, "The sequential stages of over alerting might be
evident as overreaction to minor stimuli; impaired
discrimination and evaluation of stimuli; rushes of anxiety; disorganization of behavior; and avoidance of stimuli;
particularly novelty, by withdrawing into oneself."

Autistic children also have increased levels of
norepinephrine, a substance involved in the transmission
of nerve impulses.

Whatever the reasons, I, as an autistic person, reacted
in a fixated behavior pattern in order to reduce arousal to
my overly stimulated nervous system. At puberty I was
desperate for relief from the "stage fright" nerves. I alter-
nated between erratic, impulsive behavior and withdrawal
into my inner world where stimulation could be avoided.
I even tried to avoid going on class trips because they
made me feel anxious. Sometimes intense activities such
as galloping on a horse or strenuous physical labor temporarily alleviated the attacks. But for the most part, my
life seemed to be on dead-center with these nerve attacks.
I couldn't overcome them and I couldn't escape them. I
was caught in a maze of physiological symptoms that
distressed, destroyed, and defeated any gains I had made
earlier.

CHAPTER SIX

The Door

By the time I was sixteen I was desperate for relief from the nerve attacks. The physiological symptoms seemed to accelerate with each day. Various studies I've read since described these nerve attacks as "panic anxiety" caused by my being overly sensitive to input to my nervous system from tactile and auditory senses. Intense visual input did not bother me. Dennis Charney and his co-workers at Yale University believe that there is a disorder in the system of the brain that normally inhibits excitatory nerve impulses. Today I understand this over-sensitization and how it triggers tactile defensiveness in children. But as an adolescent, the nerve attacks made me feel as if I were clinging to a greased rope suspended over an abyss.

By chance I discovered a means of temporarily easing my attacks. During the summer our school visited an amusement park. One of the rides was the Rotor, a big barrel in which people stood against the wall while it spun rapidly around and around. Centrifugal force pushed the riders to the sides of the barrel even when the floor of the barrel dropped out.

I was afraid and watched as my classmates tried out the ride. Then Lou got off the ride. "Come on, Temple. It's weird but fun." He gave me a knowing look. "You're scared, aren't you? I dare you to go."

Frightened but dared, I bought a ticket for the ride and with trembling legs, walked up the few steps to enter the barrel. My heart in my mouth, I leaned against the side. The sound of the motor starting up sent a chill skittering down my spine. Then the Rotor picked up speed and the motor sounded like a giant's hum. The colors of the blue sky, the white clouds, the yellow sun blended together like a spinning top. The smell of cotton candy, Karmel Corn, and tacos swirled around individually until they, too, combined into the carnival smell. Glued to the side of the barrel, I waited for the floor to drop out. Fear tasted bitter in my mouth and I tried to press harder against the side. With a creak of the hinges the floor opened to the ground below but now my senses were so overwhelmed with stimulation that I didn't react with anxiety or fear. I felt only the sensation of comfort and relaxation.

After the ride I was at ease with myself for the first time in a long, long time. Again and again I rode in the barrel, savoring first the over-stimulation of my senses and then the quiet surrender of my panicky, anxious nervous system. Recent studies with hyperactive children indicate that stimulating the vestibular system by spinning the child in an office chair twice weekly reduced hyper-activity.

The Rotor ride became a fixation but several weeks after the day at the amusement park, I had some uncontrollable nerve attacks. My heart pounded so hard I could see its beat through my sweater. My body felt as if it were in a sauna. My hands trembled and I could barely swallow because of the lump in my throat. My autistic logic told me there was only one answer. I had to have a Rotor ride on campus. With this fixation ruling me, I bugged the school authorities to install one. Reverting to my childhood fanciful character, Alfred Costello, I wrote frenzied communications supposedly from him to me. The following is a letter from Alfred:

Respect his letter. It is your only hope for getting help. Our school needs your Shadow representative, Temple Grandin.

I am the Shadow. For the last time take my advice. There is a reason for my signs about building a Rotor. Heed my warning before it is too late or else. Our school is doomed forever unless they build a Rotor. Mysterious forces beyond, where no one knows, govern my action. I need your help. Build a Rotor. It is the only thing that will prevent our school from falling out of existence. Right now, it is on the edge of a precarious cliff.
But if the school falls into the deep abyss of forever, you, the students, will not know a thing until you try to leave the school grounds. You will not be able to pass beyond the limits of the prop erty. You will hit a force barrier. You will be trapped for the rest of your life. I make the signs for your own good. Build a Rotor before it is too late. I do not know why building a Rotor will counteract the forces that are pushing you, the school and the staff to doom. Talk to your head master, Mr. Peters. He will think it is a crazy idea, but he will realize the truth when someday

*his car crashes into the force field. Please, please,
for the last time before it is too late. Respect the
Shadow Representative. It is for your own good. I
know know know I'm dying. Please hurry before
it is too late late late.*

The Shadow, Alfred Costello

Hurry before it is too late!

Letter number two was written several days later.

Greetings, Shadow Representative:

*Have you been following my orders to prevent
our school from falling into the dimension of
forever? Heed my advice. Build a Rotor before it
is too late. When the school fades away, you will
not know what has happened until you try to
drive past the limits of the school property. There
will be a force barrier and you will not be able to
pass through it. You will be doomed to live at
Mountain Country School forever. Never to
mingle again with the outside world. You will be
the victims of stupidity for not heeding the advice
of a superior being from across the time barrier. I
know. Heed my warning. Build a Rotor. You may
think me crazy, but the Shadow knows. After this
letter I will send one more to the Shadow's
representative, Temple Grandin. It will be the last
warning.*

Please before it is too late . . .

The Shadow, Alfred Costello

The Shadow's address:
Lunar 2
Galaxy 2

Now, even in my frenzied state, I knew the Shadow, Alfred Costello, was a figment of my imagination, a throwback to my childhood story-telling days, but I felt driven by panic anxiety to act. In rereading these letters as an adult, I find it hard to believe that I wrote them. But I did. And, as in my very young days, it was not enough to think the story. It was necessary to tell the story aloud in order for it to be real. So it was with my fixation on the Rotor ride. It was not enough to think about having such a ride on campus. I had to act out the possibility. I even went so far in promoting the carnival ride as to glue up signs on the walls of the dormitory, making quite a mess.

Fixation was my middle name. In looking back on this time of my life, I realize my behavior was similar to the perseveration of rats on amphetamines. Studies show that rats which were handled early in life had less stereotyped behavior in response to amphetamine injections than those which were not handled. Further, the study showed that rats which had been handled and then returned to their mother in the nest had less amphetamine-induced stereotype as adults than those handled and returned to the nest with no mother present. But my behavior was not artificially influenced by amphetamine injections, and the nerve attacks seemed to grow more severe and frequent. The real world had become terrifying — out of control. Each day became more unpredictable. I longed for relief, but I was trapped by physical distress. Stress showed in my speech, my actions, my relationship with others.

Then, in chapel one Sunday I sat on the folding chair, imprisoned by the school's rules of attendance and bored . . . bored . . . bored. When the minister began preaching, I escaped into my inner world of non-stimulation. A world pastel and peaceful. Suddenly a loud knock intruded upon my inner world. Startled I looked up and saw the minister rap on the lectern. "Knock," he said, "and He will answer."

Who, I wondered. I sat up straighter.

"I am the door: by me if any man enter in, he shall be saved . . . (John 10:7.9)." The minister stepped out from behind the lectern and stood in front of the congregation. He said, "Before each of you there is a door opening into heaven. Open it and be saved." He turned and walked back to the lectern. "Hymn 306, 'Bless This House.' "

I barely heard the hymn number. Like many autistic children, everything was literal to me. My mind centered on one thing. Door. A door opening to heaven. A door through which I could pass and be saved! The voices sang out and when I heard the words, "Bless this door that it may prove/Ever open to joy and love," I knew I had to find that door.

For the next few days I viewed each door as a possible opening to love and joy. The closet door, the bathroom door, the front door, the stable door—all were scrutinized and rejected as *the door*. Then one day walking back to my room from dinner, I noticed that an addition to our dorm was being constructed. The workmen had quit for the day and I walked around the new addition. There was a ladder leaning against the building and dropping my books on the ground, I climbed it to the fourth floor. A small platform extended out from the building and I climbed on it. And there was *the door!* It was a little wooden door that opened out onto the roof. I stepped into a small observation room. There were three picture windows that overlooked the mountains. I stood at one of the windows and watched the moon rise up behind the mountain range to meet the stars. A feeling of relief flooded me. For the first time in months I felt safe in the present and hope in the future. A feeling of love and joy enveloped me. I'd found it! The door to my Heaven. Thoughts that had blown through my mind randomly now seemed significant. I'd found it! A visual symbol. All I had to do was walk through that door. Of course, I didn't realize at the time that I was a visual thinker and needed concrete symbols for abstract concepts.

It was almost dark when I edged back down the ladder — a changed and searching person. I knew I had found the door to my destiny. That night I wrote in my diary: "The Crow's Nest is like a holy place. Being there, I appreciate the beauty of nature. When I look out the windows of the Crow's Nest, I feel something more. I must conquer my fears and not let them block my way."

In the days and months that followed I visited the observation room or Crow's Nest, as the carpenters called it, often. Once I entered the small room, I became calm and felt enriched with ideas and self-discoveries.

In the privacy of the Crow's Nest I thought of my childhood—the confusion, the effort to communicate, the conflicts. Now, as a teenager, communication should be established, but the chasm of misunderstanding was deep. Was it because I was autistic and my parents were not? My parents didn't understand my logic and I, being a visual thinker, did not understand theirs. Or was the chasm a universal one affecting parents and their children at different stages of life—like the teenage period? Could a bridge of love span this barrier?

Time after time I was drawn to the Crow's Nest. When I was there, I felt as if I were going to find out something about myself. And I did. I realized I was a person with fleeting whims—like the Rotor ride. And I understood for the first time what Mother had tried to tell me all

these years. Every person needs to find *her* door and open it. No one can do it for her. And the little wooden door leading to the roof and the world beyond symbolized my future. I just had to walk through it.

A year after first discovering the Crow's Nest, I stood in the small observation room and stared out the window. The night sky glittered—beckoning me to come closer. I knew I shouldn't open the little door and step out onto the roof, but I was drawn by the beauty of the night and the unknown. I unlatched the door and opened it a crack. The wind whistled through the opening like a song urging me to join it. Still I stood waiting, watching, wondering . . . Then I shoved the door open wide and stepped out into the bracing air, onto the roof, pulling the door closed behind me. I had walked into a new life and I would never spiritually go back through that old door again.

I never did. Even though I was caught sneaking up to the Crow's Nest and sent to the school psychiatrist for counseling, I had experienced an awakening of my soul and my mind. No psychiatrist was going to rob me of my newly discovered treasures.

He tried by his usual method of getting his patients fixated on him so he could control them (and continue receiving his fees), but I resisted. He said, "Temple, you know you shouldn't go up to the Crow's Nest. It's against the rules. Besides it is dangerous. Isn't that right?"

"Not to me."

"Oh, come on, Temple. What's up there?"

"Me. My life. God."

The psychiatrist laughed. "You're acting like a sailor's wife going up on a widow's walk and watching for a ship that's never going to come in. And it's never going to come in. Promise me you won't go up there again."

I didn't answer, and I didn't obey him but continued

visiting the Crow's Nest periodically. Now it wasn't only a matter of "Me. My life. God," but the added incentive of the thrill of sneaking out, climbing the ladder, flaunting the rules.

Flaunting the rules was something I hadn't outgrown. In the Crow's Nest I thought about authority and rules. When I stepped through the little wooden door onto the roof, I was beyond the school's authority. At first, I thought once the door was behind me I was beyond human authority—rules, regulations—and beyond the door was me, life, God, and freedom of choice. Then I realized that beyond the door was authority, too, but authority within one's self.

Although I was more at peace within myself, I still fought school and classes. My grades were deplorable and, worse than that, I didn't care. School was boring . . . boring . . . boring. That is, until Mr. Brooks, a psychology teacher, entered my life. He talked about animal behavior. I had always liked animals and was fascinated with Mr. Brooks' stories about them. In another lecture he showed a movie about optical illusions such as the Ames Trapezoidal Window and the Ames Distorted Room Illusion. He explained that the Distorted Room is built in such a way that it tricks one's eye. When two people of the same height stand on each side of the room, one person looks twice as tall as the other. Mr. Brooks asked me, "Can you make a room like this? I won't tell you how. I just want to see if you can figure it out."

The Distorted Room puzzle became my new fixation. For the next six months I tried to build such a room out of cardboard. At least, my fixation had been channeled into something constructive and aroused my interest in science. Obsessed by solving the Distorted Room puzzle, I began to study some of the boring subjects just in case I might learn some things that would really interest me.

But I always had time for riding, skiing, and participating in horse shows. I worked hard on making costumes for the school play and helped the workmen with construction on a new house. I was good at shingling and very proud that I could do the most complicated shingles around the flashing and the barn dormers. I still did not fit in with the other kids at school. They teased me by calling me "Bones," "Work Horse," or "Tape Recorder." This hurt.

Communicating with someone—anyone—continued to be a problem. I often sounded abrasive and abrupt. In my head I knew what I wanted to say but the words never matched my thoughts. I know now that not being able to follow the rhythm of another's speech was part of the problem and made me sound harsher than I intended. I could write my thoughts and often, while visiting the Crow's Nest, I wrote my feelings in my diary.

The little wooden door symbol was important to me and many entries deal with it. In looking back on this symbol now, I realize that the door represented my maturing and getting ready to graduate from high school. The unknown that was beyond the door was analogous to what lay beyond high school for me. Being labeled autistic didn't change the typical teenager's question—is there life after high school?

CHAPTER SEVEN

The Magical Device

What lay beyond the door for me were several caring and understanding people. Without them I might have ended up in a school for the retarded. My father had said, "Well, Temple has set a record—failed nearly every subject. Face it. Maybe she'll just have to go to a school for the retarded." Mother, bless her heart, stood up for me. Then Mr. Brooks, the psychology teacher, challenged me with the Distorted Room puzzle, which, in turn, interested me in learning—at least enough to attempt to solve the puzzle.

A second teacher, Mr. Carlock, was my salvation. Mr. Carlock didn't see any of the labels, just the underlying talents. Even the principal had doubts about my getting through tech school. But Mr. Carlock believed in building what was within the student. He channeled my fixations into constructive projects. He didn't try to draw me into his world but came instead into my world.

He seemed to sense my search for acceptance on my

own level. I trusted him implicitly. When he tried to explain the meaning of the Distorted Room, he said, "Things are not always as they appear, Temple." This enraged me because with my black and white autistic logic, I could not tolerate ambiguity. What I saw, was. I was inflexible in my opinions. Although I was always in the middle of school activities, sometimes my bizarre behavior or abrasive attitude offended. Mr. Carlock didn't preach but showed by his own conduct a social perception that I envied and tried to emulate. From him I was learning humanistic attitudes that I lacked because of my autism.

Mr. Carlock gave me philosophy books to read because he recognized that some of my thinking with symbols contained basic philosophical concepts. One day he said, "Temple, the tone of your voice has improved. It's not flat." Not flat? I puzzled about that for several days. I finally decided that as I became more socially perceptive, the tone of my voice must have improved. I guess I was no longer needing it as a defense against the world.

Years later I was shocked to learn that my speech still had minor abnormalities. I was not aware of the persistence of the hesitation and occasional flat tone of my speech. As a child growing up, instead of psychotherapy I should have received more speech therapy. Practicing with a tape recording and playing it back probably would have done more for my social life than trying to ferret out the dark secrets of my psyche. I wish one of the psychologists would have told me about my speech problem instead of worrying about my id. I was aware that sometimes people didn't want to talk to me, but I didn't know why.

Mr. Carlock was my teacher, friend, and confidant. A classmate said, "Boys don't like you, Temple. You don't have sex appeal." Crying, I repeated the comment to Mr. Carlock.

He didn't laugh or tell me not to worry. He said, "You're a gifted individual, Temple—much more than any individual with just sex appeal. Your appeal, when you grow up to it, will be not only physical but intellectual, too."

When I left Mr. Carlock's office that day, I was reassured about my worth. Because of him and other dedicated teachers and Mother's faith in me, I began to study. I had many grade points to make up but for the first time in my life I wanted to succeed in school. Mr. Carlock's interest in me motivated me to improve. Kanner conducted follow-up studies on 96 autistic children. He found that the 11 individuals who did well when they became adults, had a self-motivated change in behavior during adolescence. He writes, "Unlike most other autistic children, they may become uneasily aware of their peculiarities and begin to make a conscious effort to do something about them." Mr. Carlock had sensed that I had reached a stage for possible change/advancement and with his caring attitude motivated me to reach out—to learn.

During the summer after my junior year in high school, I visited my Aunt Ann on her ranch in Arizona. She, too, helped me immensely. When Mother first suggested I spend the vacation with my aunt, I didn't want to go. After all, except for a few weekend visits at home, I had not been away from the school. This was a standard policy. Mr. Peters, director of Mountain Country School, felt that controlled and unchanging environment was not only beneficial but essential. Going to the ranch would mean coping with a new environment in addition to traveling with its hazardous exposure to different people, places, situations—all of which could trigger nerve attacks for me.

There were two choices in coping with the nerve problem: I could retreat into my inner world and minimize the stimulation or I could fight fire with fire — find the most stimulating activity and "go for it." I remembered how over stimulation from the carnival Rotor ride had helped to relieve my nerves. The ride's intense overpowering form of tactile and vestibular stimulation superceded my tendency to avoid vestibular and tactile stimulation. There was absolutely no way I could resist. Afterwards I had felt peace within for a brief time. At the ranch there would be no carnival ride to stimulate me, but there would be horses to gallop strenuously and intense physical labor.

Once at the ranch I talked and talked and talked about the Ames Distorted Room. Again and again I told Ann how the room was built on angles, and the story of my struggle to solve this puzzle and how finally, Mr. Brooks, the psychology teacher, had given me a psychology book with a diagram of the room. Although my many cardboard models of the Distorted Room hadn't solved the puzzle, each new model I had made was closer to the solution. I studied the diagram and finally built a small Distorted Room illusion from plywood. Fixated on my struggle and eventual success, I repeated the story again and again to Ann. She was kind, patient, and listened to my fixation — over and over. It must have driven her absolutely crazy.

Like Mr. Brooks she tried to direct my fixation tendency into something constructive. She suggested I rebuild the roof of the pump house, repair a railing on a fence, help with the cattle in the squeeze chute — a device for holding an animal for branding, vaccination, or castration.

Doing physical labor eased my nerve attacks, and I

was fascinated by the workings of the squeeze chute. The animal was driven into this device and its head positioned into the headgate, a piece of equipment similar to the pillory used as punishment in Pilgrim times. The squeeze chute had steel and wood sidepanels, which were hinged on the bottom to form a V. After the animal was in the enclosure and his head locked into the headgate, the chute operator pulled a rope, which pulled the panels, which then pressed against the sides of the animal. This

pressure prevented the animal from moving about or slipping down and choking itself in the headgate. I watched wild-eyed and nervous calves, one by one, being driven into the squeeze chute. A few minutes after the panels put pressure on either side those same wild-eyed, nervous animals calmed down. Why? Did the gentle pressure comfort and ease the over-stimulated nerves of the calf? If so, would such a gentle pressure help me?

For hours I watched as the fearful and twitchy animals were locked into the cattle chute, and after the panels were pressed gently against their sides, saw them calm down. Finally, I asked Aunt Ann to let me try the cattle chute. The pressure helped the calves, maybe it would help me. First, I adjusted the headgate to accommodate the height of my head when on my hands and knees and then I climbed into the enclosure. Ann pulled the rope which pulled the sides of the squeeze chute together. Soon I felt their firm pressure on my sides. Ordinarily, I would have withdrawn from such pressure as from the engulfing embrace of my overweight, marshmallowy relative during childhood days. But in the cattle chute withdrawal wasn't possible. No way could I avoid the pressure unless I was released from the squeeze chute.

The effect was both stimulating and relaxing at the same time. But most importantly for an autistic person, I was in control—unlike being swallowed by an over-affectionate relative, I was able to direct Ann as to the comfortable degree of pressure. The squeeze chute provided relief from my nerve attacks. True to form, I became fixated on it.

After my summer vacation, Aunt Ann wrote
Mother:

*. . . As you know, I awaited Temple's ar-
rival at the ranch with a mixture of anticipa-
tion and apprehension. You'd told me how
she'd get zeroed in on an idea and be reluc-
tant to leave it. I'd heard of her violent
temper if rules were too stringent. Since I
was essentially innocent of "rules" except
what was dictated by reason and common
sense—I never saw the temper. You'd told
me she was very handy and she was! How
fortunate for me since I am of all things
unhandy and the ranch always has projects
crying out for someone good with tools to
carry them out. And Temple was more than
willing. I bought leather and silver trim.
Temple made silver-mounted bridles. Our
kids wanted to have informal horseshows.
Temple fearlessly and competently assumed
the role of ringmaster and judge. We were
badly in need of a gate over a non-functional
cattleguard—one which could be opened
without getting out of the car. Using matches
and thread Temple constructed a model,
figuring dimensions and weights, and subse-
quently built us a full-sized gate which could
be opened by pulling a rope from the car. It
swings open, propelled by the rope and
weights and allows time for the passage of a
car, then closes again.
On the debit side she did, as advertised,
get on one subject and ride it to death.
Temple deals in symbols and when she finds*

*one which would, so to speak, bear the
weight of some of her fears and frustrations,
she never lets go of it. The "door" which
stood for venturing forth into new realms
and endeavors, I heard about until I could
tell the story verbatim. Several times I interrupted in the middle of her subject. She
allowed me to finish my interjection and then
resumed* her *story exactly where she'd left
off. Yes, it was a little aggravating but
Temple is so basically sensible, so obviously
intelligent and so willing to help with any
problem we had, that listening to her was a
small price to pay.*

*The cattle chute, which I'm sure you've
heard about, was a symbol which reconciled
two opposing drives—the urge to submit to
and enjoy tactile restraint and the opposing
reluctance to allow anyone, even you, her
mother, and certainly not the overpowering
aunt, to provide. I admit I did not understand Temple's preoccupation with the cattle
chute. In fact, I had some very bad moments
standing by while she was held in the cattle
chute. While she was apparently experiencing
a good sensation, I was wondering feverishly
what I was going to say to the ranch foreman
if he should happen along and ask what we
were doing. Whether I understand the
fascination or not, I did see that the chute
was in some way very important to
Temple—a symbol very useful to her in
working out her own solutions to problems.
For this reason I vigorously defend it. And if
Temple later builds a prototype for her own*

use, fine. Far from being an unhealthy sort of thing, I feel it is simply part of the way in which her unusual mind works out its unusual problems.

I am proud to have had even a small part in freeing that good brain for the constructive work I know she can do. I know there'll come a day when I will very joyously say, "I knew her when . . . "

Love,
Ann Brecheen

When I returned to school that fall, I was still fixated on the squeeze chute. Mr. Carlock directed my fixation into a constructive project. With his advice I built a squeeze chute-like device out of scrap wood. My squeeze

chute project concerned the school psychologist, who said, "Well, Temple, I haven't decided whether this contraption of yours is a prototype of the womb or a casket." He laughed.

"Neither," I said.

He shifted in his chair. Then, clearing his throat, he leaned across the desk as though sharing a secret. "*We* do not have an identity problem here, do *we*? I mean, *we* don't think we're a cow or something, do *we*?"

"Are you crazy or something? Of course, I don't think I'm a cow or something. Do you think *you're* a cow?"

The talk with the psychologist ended with his losing his temper. "You've done some bizarre things here at Mountain Country School, Temple, and the staff has tried to have empathy and understanding. But this squeeze box—it's weird. I have no choice but to advise your mother of my opinion."

The psychiatry department, too, thought my project was strange—sick—and I shouldn't use it. They even went so far as to try to take it away from me, which only made me more prone to nerve attacks. The school convinced Mother that my using the squeeze chute was bad for me. This became a bone of contention between us and drove me, even more, to prove that the relaxing effect the squeeze chute had on me might also have the same effect on other people. It just wasn't some figment of my weird mind. It was real. For the first time in my life I felt a purpose for learning—a reason beyond solving the Distorted Room puzzle—a real reason. Why did the pressure of the cattle chute calm frightened calves and soothe nerve-driven me?

Often, sitting in the Crow's Nest, I pondered this question and my fate. Whatever the future held for me, I knew it involved stepping through the little wooden door, symbol of salvation, joy, and happiness. The door. The door. The door. What lay beyond it was what I made it. I had to trust in myself before I could make others trust in me and my thoughts. And I had many fearful thoughts — some about sex. I tried to push them out, to pretend they didn't exist, but they did.

Many times in the squeeze chute I had pleasurable sensations and thoughts about love. As a child I had wished for a small cubby hole about three feet wide and three feet high. The squeeze chute I ultimately built was that secret, coveted cubby hole of childhood dreams. Sometimes I worried that the squeeze chute would overpower me, and I would not be able to survive without it. Then I realized that the chute was just a restrictive device made from scrap plywood. It was a product of my mind. The same feelings and thoughts I had in the chute could be had outside of it. The thoughts were creations of my mind — not of the squeeze chute. When I was in the chute, I felt closer to people like Mother, Mr. Peters, Mr. Brooks, Mr. Carlock, and Aunt Ann. Although the squeeze chute was just a mechanical device, it broke through my barrier of tactile defensiveness, and I felt the love and concern of these people and was able to express my feelings about myself and others. It was as if an accordion folding door had been shoved back revealing my emotions.

When I first built the chute, it was similar to the one at the ranch. I was locked in and released by another person. This did not work well at school so I fixed the chute so I could lock myself in or release myself. The squeeze chute not only allowed me to express my feelings, but since I wouldn't allow myself the relaxation/stimulation of the chute until my homework was completed, the squeeze chute served as an incentive.

Finally, the day I would walk through the first of

many doors arrived. Graduation Day! I was chosen to give one of the several speeches.

Commencement Speech
June 12, 1966

In everybody's life there comes a time when one stops being a child and walks through a door to be on one's own. It was three years ago when I first broadened my outlook concerning my future. On the fourth floor of our newly constructed main house there is a small three-sided room known as the Crow's Nest that overlooks the countryside. One night, returning to my room from dinner, I noticed a ladder leaning against the construction and I climbed it and entered the observation room. I stared out into the snowy, windy night through the frosty icicle-framed windowpane and I realized that I'd found a place where I could be alone with my inner, solitary thoughts and at peace with myself. It was here that I began thinking about my future after I left this school. A small wooden door leading out onto the roof symbolized my step into the future. I thought that when I walked through that door onto the roof I was my own authority.

To be able to walk through the little door one must be mature enough to handle the challenges and responsibilities that have to be faced. One must also have faith in oneself and faith in others. There are many times when one must trust other people. One must go to these situations without fearful apprehension because faith will conquer fear.

Now that I have worked on my aunt's ranch in Arizona and faced nature's realities, I feel I have already passed through that little door. I was my own authority at the ranch. This is how I went through the little door. I asked my aunt to put me in a cattle squeeze chute that would render me completely helpless, utterly unable to escape from it. I had to have faith in her as my friend that she would not go away and leave me in the cattle chute. As I walked down the narrow alley towards the squeeze chute, I wanted to run away to avoid being squeezed by the steel sides of the chute. I had to walk in calmly and quietly and not scream and struggle when the lever that would close a metal yoke around my neck was pushed down. I knew that I had to face the fact that I could not run away from the threshold of the little door. I stepped up a slight incline into the cattle chute. I had a panicky urge to jump out before the steel bars entrapped me. But I controlled myself and did not bang against the sides.

When I brought myself to be able to ask calmly and quietly to be released, my Aunt Ann released the squeeze panels and I was free. Early this year I realized that if one is to get anything worth while out of anything, one must put at least a small amount of individual energy. Energy is needed to release more energy. Going through that door symbolized my decision to pull up my marks and really work hard. This door was the first stage of that long hard climb to my academic goal of graduating from this school. To graduate is like climbing a ladder to the door in the sky. Every good grade is another rung towards the top. I figuratively climbed a ladder to a door that is four floors up on the side of the main house. I stood at the bottom of the ladder and wondered how I would ever get there. Slowly I climbed, forcing myself rung by rung up the ladder until I reached the door. When I stood in front of that door I knew I could make it. I knew I could graduate.

Today I am at the top of the ladder and am about to walk through that door to my future. I feel in my heart more now than ever before the kindness and love that Mr. and Mrs. Peters have given me to help me reach this point in my life. I know I shall always be thankful to them and remember them as I climb my next ladder to the top. In passing through this symbolic door, I think of the words of the beautiful song, "You Will Never Walk Alone," from "Carousel."

Today, more than ever, I realize I have not walked alone here at Mountain Country School. I thank not only the staff at the school, but my family and friends as well.

CHAPTER EIGHT

Through the Little Door

After graduating from Mountain Country School I visited Aunt Ann on her Arizona ranch again. I felt comfortable—unstressed—because I was returning to familiar people in a familiar place and doing familiar ranch tasks. Soon after I arrived, Mother wrote:

Dear Temple:

How exciting about Ann's horse having a colt. Give it a special pat on the nose from me. I must say your description of branding did sound pretty sickening. I don't think I could do it.

You know, I was thinking about our conversation on love and wondering how one would put down on paper what love is. It seems to me that love is wanting to make things grow and having a stage in their growth. First, one wants to grow oneself and one develops symbols in order to do this. Think of your cattle chute. In the beginning you made it because you were bored and homesick for the ranch. Then, as you put your effort into it, it began to stand for the maturity you had acquired out West — that step through the door. In other words, your desire to grow. Wanting to grow is really loving yourself, loving the best part of yourself. And so this love is represented by the cattle chute (and then, too, your need for physical love gets tied up in the cattle chute as well). After one learns to love oneself, one begins to want to take care of the same instinct in other people so that they can grow too — so that they can step through their little door. As soon as one puts effort into making someone or something grow, one begins to have a stake in that someone or something. You have a stake in the ranch because you have worked on it. I have a stake in the house here because I've worked on it. We would hate to see these places destroyed because we love them. People have a stake in each other too. I love you because I have invested so much of myself in you and I want to see you grow. But how do you feel about me?

Here's the difference. Human beings are alive and respond. Objects cannot speak to you or hug you. Objects are only something made out of imagination and energy and raw materials. They can only mean whatever meaning we give them. A human isn't a private symbol or a representation of our effort, but a living creature who answers us.

We may not always like the answer. It may be different from what we expect, but this answering creature has a soul—a soul struggling to perfect itself just as ours is. This creature is unique just as we are. Never in all the eons of existence will there be another like it. Now you could say the same thing about a snowflake or a kitten, but there is something more in the uniqueness of humans. We are dream creatures. You and I each has our dream of perfection and in the sharing of our dream we learn from the other. As we work together, we develop a stake in each other. We not only "love" but are "loved" in return. Objects cannot love you. Animals' love is limited, but human beings become deeply involved with each other. Even if they hate each other, they are involved. Love doesn't necessarily have a special feeling within. It's really just being committed to each other and listening to each other and learning from each other. And then, somewhere along the way, without our really knowing when, we find that we "care" and that if we lost this person, we would mind the loss . . .

Dear Mother. So loving. So caring. Her concern veiled in subtleties. But I knew what she meant by a kitten or a snowflake not being special like another human. Mother still couldn't reconcile herself to my using the prototype of the cattle chute. The school psychologists had done a good job in convincing her that the chute was bad—something to be discouraged. This disagreement over the use of my comfort machine drove me, even more, to prove that the relaxing effect the cattle chute had on me could also work with other people. It wasn't just a figment of my weird mind. It was real.

When I left the ranch at the end of the summer, I entered college. I will forever bless those who selected a small college for me. Had I entered a large university, I would have been lost in the maze of many buildings and thousands of students. Even though I got the honored reputation for being the best lock-picker on campus (many a locker I opened for forgetful friends), I started to develop some friendships.

The college, fortunately, was near Mountain Country School. And, Mr. Carlock, my salvation, was still around encouraging me. When I told him about the flack I was getting from psychologists and Mother about my machine, he said wisely, "Well, let's build a better one and do some scientific experiments with college students. Let's find out if the squeeze machine really does relax. Find out if the effect is, indeed, real."

"Okay. Where do we start?" I asked.

"We start with you, Temple," Mr. Carlock said firmly and then smiled. "If you want to prove your theory, then you'll have to learn math, read scientific articles in the library, do some research." I took his advice and learned to use the scientific indexes and to read and understand technical journal articles. Every weekend Mr. Carlock came over and took me to his laboratory workshop to work on the squeeze machine.

He aroused my interest in science and directed my fixation into a worthy project. I spent hours at the library looking up everything I could find on the effect sensory input into one sense system had on sensory perception in another sensory system. To my amazement I discovered that there was a whole field of study called sensory interaction. Eventually, my undergraduate thesis was concerned with sensory interaction and experiments I did with the squeeze machine (cattle chute). The results of my experiments indicated that the pressure stimulus affected auditory thresholds.

After much research and study I built "PACES," my second prototype of the squeeze machine. PACES stood for Pressure Apparatus Controlled Environment Sensory. This model with its foam-padded panels was a Cadillac compared to my first Spartan wooden cattle chute. Of course, because the staff and the psychologists had all been exposed to the Freudian school of thought, they attributed all kinds of sexual implications to my cattle chute. This made me feel guilty.

Still, I reasoned, using the machine couldn't be all bad. At college I was making great strides in communicating with people. I attributed this "break-through" in getting along better with people to my maligned squeeze machine. It enabled me to learn to be gentle, to have empathy, to know that gentleness is not synonymous with weakness. I was learning how to feel. Two case studies of high-functioning autistic adults indicated that lack of empathy was one of their greatest deficiencies. One man wrote that he did not care about people. Other young adults who have recovered from autism have had difficulty relating to other people. An autistic man wrote, "I was very cold hearted, too. It was impossible for me to give or receive love from anybody. I often repulsed it by turning people off. That's still a problem today—relating to other people. I like things over people and didn't care about people at all." Jules R. Bemporad, Harvard Medical School, describes another autistic adult: "Jerry appears at times to understand intellectually how another person might feel, but he does not seem to be able to automatically sense himself in another's inner state."

Feeling the soothing pressure from the squeeze machine slowly enabled me to start to have feelings of empathy. I wrote in my diary: "Children have to be taught to be gentle. Since I missed out on this, I have to learn it now. The squeeze chute gives the feeling of being held, cuddled and gently cradled in Mother's arms. This is hard to write down. Writing it down is a form of accepting the feeling."

Research with baby monkeys has indicated that if they do not receive enough contact comfort, they have a weakened capacity for future affection. It is likely that in order to have feelings of caring, one has to have experienced the feeling of comfort. Animal experiments reveal that comforting tactile stimulation causes distinct biochemical changes in the central nervous system. I speculate that regular use of the squeeze machine may help change some of the abnormal biochemistry which was caused by the lack of comforting tactile stimulation during my early childhood. Maybe the lack of empathy in many autistic adults is caused by their avoidance of hugging and affection when they were children. However, it cannot be emphasized too strongly that the squeeze machine is *not* recommended as a panacea for all autistic children.

The pressure of the new cattle chute was gentle, but it could not be resisted. Therefore, the pressure was more powerful by being gentle. Because I had to force myself to accept the chute and the pressure of its panels—and most importantly, because I was in control of the amount of pressure—I was finally beginning to be able to endure brief physical contacts like a pat on the shoulder or a handshake.

Even though I recognized the benefits of the cattle chute, I was still afraid of it. I feared the sexual implications others hinted at. But then I realized the real fear was the fear of looking at myself and being confined with me. I realized that in spite of the sexual connotations others attributed to the device, my thoughts and fantasies were not the fault of the "evil" machine. The cattle chute was merely an amplifier and it was no more responsible for my thoughts than a record player was responsible for the music on the record.

I felt that once the cattle chute was accepted by others as beneficial, I would believe more strongly in myself. Full acceptance was looking deep within myself and not being able to defend, rationalize, or protect myself from its effect. Ever since I was very young, I had dreamed of an enclosure that would give me comfort. I also sensed, even at that young age, that whatever device I built would enable me to understand and think in realms unexplored by others. I wondered if I would become dependent on such a device. The cattle chute was something I believed in and built. I was learning to control myself in the chute and not fight the pressure. If I accepted the pressure and relaxed, it calmed and soothed me.

Test results on other people using the squeeze machine indicated that the squeeze machine tended to lower some metabolic functions. Out of 40 normal college students, 62 percent liked the squeeze machine and found it to be relaxing. The squeeze machine applied pressure to the body areas most sensitive for eliciting the "skin pressure reflex" in man. Some people found that the squeeze machine was relaxing for the first 10 or 15 minutes and then it became annoying. There may be an optimal level of stimulation. The squeeze machine was found to be less effective on hot summer days or if the room was cold. So my fixation on the cattle chute not only benefitted me, but was relaxing for 62 percent of the 40 college students participating in the experiment. I felt justified in my cattle chute fixation.

The squeeze machine is currently being used at a clinic which treats autistic and hyperactive children and adults. Lorna King, an occupational therapist who is director of the Center for Neurodevelopmental Studies in Phoenix, Arizona, finds the device is helpful in reducing hyperactivity. She reports that a hyperactive adult, using the squeeze machine for twenty minutes, felt and acted much calmer the next day. Although Lorna King has had success treating some autistic children with sensory integration therapy, stimulation is never forced on a child. Vestibular, deep pressure, and other tactile stimulation are applied to help the damaged nervous system repair itself. Sensory stimulation will cause new neural circuits to form. Rats housed in an enriched environment with many toys and things to climb on had greater neuronal growth in the brain than rats kept in standard lab cages. Vestibular stimulation may help speed up maturation of the nervous system. Dogs subjected to vestibular and tactile stimulation had larger vestibular neurons.

Using doors as symbols was another fixation and one I carried from high school into college. Actually stepping through a doorway was my means of acting out a decision—like graduating from high school and planning for college. Going through a physical door made abstract decisions real. Symbolically, my door fixation marked the passages in the corridor of time. Because my learning strength was visual, this acting out was a logical extension of that ability.

After two years of study at college, I again began to contemplate the future—graduation and then graduate school. Emotional preparation and acting out the symbolic excursion into this future was essential, and again I sought the symbolic door through which to pass. A trap door leading to the roof of the dormitory signified passage into new territory. Of course, climbing through the trap door and out onto the roof was forbidden, which only added to the significance of the act. Anything worth doing has its hazards, and the illegality of the act added to my commitment to the future. If it were safe and legal to pass through the door, then it would not be realistic for me. This excursion would be my first conscious breaking of college rules, but I knew I had to go through that door in order to make the possibility of commencement and then graduate school more than a vague, dreamy cloud in my mind. So again, as in high school, I passed through the forbidden door. I poked my head through the trap-door and peeked out across the roof. The air was windy and wet. As I looked out across the land, the moon broke through the clouds. Until I graduated, I continued to use the trap door to reinforce my decisions on the future. The trap door represented difficult-to-explain feelings and was a hands-on symbol for my intangible idea. Opening a specific door was a concrete expression of my decision to achieve. After I went through the door, I pulled up my marks in high school. Actually, going through the door was sort of like signing a contract to improve myself. It made my decision seem real.

There is not a doubt in my mind that the cattle chute and my symbolic door were instrumental in my improved scholastic endeavors and my relationships with people. I still had some problems with social relationships. Some students called me "Buzzard Woman!" Even when I wore stylish clothes, many students did not want to talk to me. I couldn't figure out what I was doing wrong. A big step forward in social development was working as part of a team on "The Raven Review," the school's talent show—a giant step forward from my early school years when my main contact with my peers was to hit them. I built and painted almost half the sets used in the show. My peers respected my creative abilities. It was easier to make contact with other people while doing an activity we all were interested in.

The summer following my junior year at college, I worked at a hospital with emotionally disturbed children. Seven-year-old Jake was one of the children at this institution. He intrigued me because I saw some of me in him. As I used to wrap pieces of plastic around me as a child, Jake, even in the hot summer, wrapped a blanket around himself. Although Jake was not classified as autistic, he did have some of the characteristics of autism. Most of the time he was indifferent toward people — not looking directly at them nor listening to them. He was fixated on mechanical objects. Although he could talk normally, often he would scream or yell if he were asked to do something such as "Sit down, Jake." That summer I spent a lot of time with him talking about mechanical things. I began to feel as if I were Mr. Carlock, opening up doors to Jake's secret world. Sometimes, I was able to get through to him about people. But it was a matter of talking first about his fixation — mechanical gadgets — and then easing people into the conversation. Otherwise, Jake would not communicate at all.

As a rule therapists object to catering to fixations. But many fixations in autistic-type children have to do with a need for reducing arousal in an over-active nervous system. By concentrating on the fixation, they block out other stimulation which they cannot handle. Repetitive, monotonous stimulation may reduce neural firing in normal adults. Too many therapists and psychologically-trained people believe that if the child is allowed to indulge his fixations, irreparable harm will be done. I do not believe this is true in all cases. Fixations are nothing more than traits that are extreme. A child might be stubborn, but when that trait becomes all-consuming, the trait is labeled fixation. Certain traits are beneficial. Stubbornness is related to perseverance, and perseverance is a good trait and necessary for reaching certain goals. The traits in an autistic are the same traits as in a normal individual, but in an autistic some of the traits have gone haywire.

I remember when I was young, I sort of liked stimulation that was painful. So it might be with kids who mutilate themselves. Perhaps they could be directed into a more positive, less destructive form of self-stimulation. And possibly my "machine" could help these youngsters. Maybe if the child learned to like the stimulation from the squeeze machine, he would not bite his fingers. Recent research on animals indicates that self-stimulation and stereotyped behavior will reduce arousal in frustrated animals. The stereotyped behavior lowered cortisol (stress hormone) levels. Autistic children have an overactive nervous system. The symptoms of autism and sensory deprivation are similar. People and animals that are sensorily deprived have an overly sensitized nervous system resulting in lowered thresholds to sensory stimuli.

Perhaps if a child used the squeeze machine, he could apply intense yet pleasant stimulation to himself. Since the chute is designed to feel very much like being held by a person, it might help the child learn to like being held or touched by a person. Once the child can operate the chute and likes it, the next step would be human affection. The chute is an important step because the child controls it.

Obviously, if a child is mutilating his body, he has to be stopped. But other types of fixations should not always be discouraged. They can be the means of communicating, as in Jake's case. Turning a negative act into a positive one is possible. Also, I believe that Jake would have been helped immeasurably by my squeeze machine. I have been corresponding with an adult autistic woman.

She has difficulty controlling her temper. In her letters her craving for tactile stimulation is apparent. She uses tactile words to describe things—words like fluffy and soft. She likes the idea of the squeeze machine. Perhaps the squeeze machine would help her.

But my using the squeeze machine was a bone of contention among therapists, friends, and relatives. They even tried to take it away from me. In the long run they did harm because they made me feel guilty as though using the machine was nasty and sick. It took many years for me to overcome this guilt trip and completely accept the machine.

On the other hand, when they tried to take the machine away from me, it made me work harder to prove that the machine had a practical and beneficial use. Their disapproval drove me to do something constructive with my fixation on cattle chutes.

My fixation on doors continued through college. In my diary I confessed my fears for my future. I worried about whether I was prepared. I was eager to step through the symbolic door into new experiences. Sometimes at the college I felt as if I were in a prison. In a way I was—my own prison—unless I was willing to study, to gain self-control, to get along with people, and take that step through the door to freedom and the future. Life was a circle and I knew the past could not be left behind. The symbolic door at college was nothing more than an extension of the Crow's Nest at boarding school and represented living and communicating. And the cattle chute was a means of learning about my emotions. Neither living nor learning was good without the other.

College days were coming to an end. Finals and then graduation! I had worked hard on my studies; I had made great strides in getting along with my peers; I felt the beginnings of harmony within. One of the last papers I wrote for the marriage and family class expressed my frustrations and fears, my hopes and dreams:

The final is to write a paper about my hopes and aims in marriage. I could give you two pages of theoretical ideas about the perfect marriage or tell you the truth about me. I think it is stupid and foolish to write a paper full of bull, because you'll know it's bull. To get down to brass tacks the theoretical idea of marriage is not my ideal—who can live in theory anyway. I am hesitant to write my real feelings because it can be risky. Many times I have been burned because I revealed my secrets and they were blabbed all over the campus and generally misunderstood. If I cannot trust you, I'll probably never be able to trust anyone. I have decided to tell the truth on this paper. After you've read it, I would appreciate it if you would return it to me or destroy it so that unauthorized personnel will not have the opportunity to find out my top military secrets. NOW THE REAL NITTY GRITTY!

My purpose for being on this planet is to build a device or develop a method that can be used to teach people how to look at themselves and to be gentle and caring. I feel that this is very important because I had to build a device to teach me to feel for others. Throughout my entire life my thoughts churned on how I could build a machine that would teach me to feel gentleness. I have now built part of that machine, a prototype of the cattle chute.

Ever since I was a child, I have been a person, up until just a few years ago, who was completely turned on by machines instead of

112

people. I closed myself off from people and didn't even speak until I was four years old. There is a highfalutin' name for this condition—autism. Even yet, I am turned on by machines, especially control mechanisms designed to interact with people.

It was through the use of the cattle chute, a device I have been designing in my head since early childhood, that I taught myself how to feel. I spent hours in school thinking about the miraculous device instead of studying. I did not start to study until I realized that knowledge was necessary in order to build the device which would apply the stimulus I lacked as a youngster.

You are probably asking what all this has to do with the feeling of purpose. Plenty. God, whatever that is, and chance formed the gene structure that made me and something happened in the process which disconnected the "wire" in the brain that attracts a child to its mother and other humans offering affection. It was not until I was old enough and skilled enough to build the squeeze machine that the connection was repaired. Maybe God or destiny willed it that way so I would invent a method or device that would help other people. The only way that the inventer can be sure his device works is to use it on himself successfully.

Even now, after I have built and used the squeeze machine, I still reject it and am afraid of it. The feeling of being in the cattle chute is gentle but the feelings it arouses are often painful. I still have difficulty accepting my emotional side. One of the major reasons for my fear is the anxiety that my emotions will over-come me and I will not fulfill my destiny. This is why I fear marriage. It is more important for me to build the device or develop the method to help other people than for me to be "normal" and marry.

In a marriage the girl is subservient. I have not seen one marriage yet that could be a model one for me. The only way I could marry would be if my husband and I worked as scientists.

Regretfully, there still is prejudice against women in this society—even on this campus. The administration treats the women on their staff as if they were stupid. They have little or no respect for them. It is this bigoted attitude which has turned me off marriage and made me become a celibate person.

One point I want to make clear is that the purpose of the squeeze machine is not to make a person submit to some doctrine put out by society but rather to enable the person to com-pletely search his soul and come to terms with his intellect—maybe enable the person to get a little closer to God and not always be thinking about his own personal gain. If the only way I could get my device used around the world before I die would be to have somebody steal it and get all the credit, I would let them.

But alas like B.F. Skinner in Walden Two *I do not want to submit to my own invention, especially before it is all over the country. Only after that can I jump in too. I would have been nothing if I had not clung to this idea all my life. It is the only thing that gives me the motivation to study hard in school. I get frustrated when I cannot do math because math is needed to build the device.*

Well, Mr. Weber, this is the real paper not just two pages of beautifully manicured bull, but three pages of sloppy, mispelled, poorly typed, written truth. *A bull paper on this topic means nothing. I hope I can trust you not to discuss any aspects of this paper with anyone.*

Mr. Weber wrote on this paper: "Excellent. Thank you. You are always original and thoughtful. I am always confidential with such 'insights.' "

Then the big day came. Class of '70. Graduation from college with a B.A. in psychology and Salutatorian of my class.

It was now time to walk through the door into my future. I had reached the top of the college ladder and now was at the bottom rung of graduate school.

After graduation ceremonies I went through the trap door onto the roof. I felt confident. I placed a plaque on the roof of the library, commemorating my advance through another door of life. The plaque was inscribed with the words *"Saxum, Atruim, Culman,"* which translates very roughly to "Strive for the threshold of the top." I had conquered the college ladder and was ready to begin the ascent of the graduate school ladder.

The word "commencement" means beginning. Through the door and onto the roof top was my symbolic beginning for graduate school. To remind me of my success, Mother gave me a gold charm with the inscription "Through the Little Door."

CHAPTER NINE

Graduate School and the Glass Door Barrier

The summer after graduating from college I spent at home. During this time I built a new cattle chute. It worked much better than previous versions. It had several refinements such as more comfortable padding and a padded headrest.

Through the use of my squeeze machine I learned to control my aggression and to accept affection. Sometimes I would have periods when the nerve attacks subsided. During these nerve free periods I suffered from eczema and colitis. There were times when the colitis attacks were so severe, I ate only yogurt and Jello for three weeks. In order to correct these disorders, I needed to feel intense emotion to ease my nerves. My new cattle chute was much easier to give into and accept. Aggressive, negative thoughts were difficult because the soothing feeling made aggression melt away. I could only be comfortable in the machine if I let go and relaxed.

Often I felt ambivalent towards the cattle chute. I

realized I feared the cattle chute because in it I was ruled by my emotions. This was good because if I didn't feel pleasurable, positive emotion, my aggressive, negative emotion took over. The more I accepted my emotions, the more I was able to really feel and care for other people.

Even the cat liked me more now. I guess it was getting good vibes from me. Perhaps I had to be comforted myself by the squeeze machine before I could give comfort to the cat.

Still, with all my bravado about accepting the cattle chute, I was anxious about using it if Mother was in the next room. Even though she had read my thesis with the cattle chute test results and had approved of it, I still sensed her reservations. I wanted her to try my new prototype, but she put it off with one excuse or another.

In September I moved to Arizona and began graduate school in the psychology program. This should have been my time for self-approval and self-praise. After all, I had come a long way from the non-verbal, tantrum-throwing, peer-hitting child. Instead, I was filled with self-doubts and a sense of worthlessness. The fixation to find meaning in my life drove me relentlessly. This fixation fueled by the panic anxiety attacks consumed me. My biggest fear was that I would have a huge nerve attack in public. Fixating on something reduced the arousal level of my nervous system. This time my fixation wasn't an ordinary door like the one in the Crow's Nest or a trapdoor as at college, but an automatic, sliding glass door. So simple and yet so complex. Over and over I asked myself why this sliding glass door obsessed me. In my life going through a door signified a step forward for me. Why my hang-up on this door?

One difference was the legality of the sliding glass door. Using the other symbolic doors held the thrill of accomplishing an illegal act without being caught. This supermarket door was used by thousands of shoppers. Still, when I faced that door, I became physically ill. My legs trembled, my forehead beaded with perspiration, and my stomach churned. I rushed the door, hoping to leave the creeping sickness behind, but it followed me. Once on the other side of the door I leaned against the side of the building, my heart pounding, my body shivering with nerves, and nausea enveloping me. I began to think about breaking the sliding glass door — put it out of *my* misery. I tried to think logically about this fixation. What was the attraction and why was I fearful? Wasn't it just a damn plain sliding glass door?

Then I thought of another difference about this door. Openness. There was no secrecy. I wrote in my diary: "It's just a glass door. But still it's a barrier. I guess the significance lies in the two seconds it takes to pass through it. Like changing from one mental state to another. No matter how many times I go back and forth I'm still in the same environment. But my perception of that environment changes. If a person changes his state of mind, he just changes it. The environment does not change. No mystery!"

Three weeks after wrestling with the sliding glass door fixation, I finally went through the door like a regular shopper. I didn't rush it. I just walked through and it was a pretty groovy experience. In the next few weeks I visited the supermarket often. One day I went back and forth through the sliding glass door ten times. The only thing I feared was ridicule. The manager of the store noticed me, but, fortunately, he did not say anything.

But it wasn't only my fixation on the sliding glass door that distressed me. Using my cattle chute haunted me. Outwardly I acknowledged its benefits but inwardly I denied its rough and harsh origin. It was difficult to integrate cattle chutes that were used on animals with the ones that I had built. One of the reasons for this was that cattle had to have many painful things done to them and thus the cattle chute appeared cruel. Once in awhile someone would be deliberately cruel to the animal in the chute, but, as a rule, the animals were not treated meanly. Basically, the cattle chute was just a holding device so that they could be branded or vaccinated. The whole concept involved being held.

When I first used the real cattle chute, I was locked in the headgate; then I built a hard, wooden one for my use which felt like the ones used on animals. When I could bear being held, I modified my cattle chute so that it would be gentle.

Until I could come to terms with this benefit/rejection paradox, I couldn't even look at a cattle chute advertisement without flinching from the thoughts and emotions which surfaced. It was only after I took a picture of me in a real cattle chute and had it made into a poster and mounted that I faced my fears. I finally was getting to the point where I thought of my cattle chute with pleasure and affection. This enabled me to have a friendlier attitude toward other people. I even started referring to *my* cattle chute. Still, sometimes in the shadows of my mind, I knew fear — fear of my thoughts and emotions while in the cattle chute.

Then the Arizona State Fair opened and I had to face several realities. Seven years ago I had ridden on the Rotor carnival ride and became obsessed with it. Studies show that often autistic children are fearful of rapid movements at first and then become fixated on them. Now I went on the ride again and a few more puzzle pieces fell into place. Research reveals that autistic children, as a rule, like intense stimulation — even stimuli that might be perceived as painful to normal children. The desire for intense stimulation may be what causes some autistic children to self mutilate. Suddenly I was aware that the Rotor ride was not only a precursor to my cattle chute, but it was about twice as rough as the original cattle chute. The Rotor literally plastered me against the wall by its force. I had no choice but to give in to its sensation. Even though the wall of the barrel dug into my back and hurt, I realized for the first time that it had taken something as violent acting as the Rotor ride to first break through my defenses and make me feel. After the carnival ride I passed a cattle chute display. Thoughts and emotions flooded my nervous system. I stepped back from the display, afraid. As the tactile defensiveness broke down and I grew older, the intense stimulation of the Rotor was painful and made me feel sick. When I first started using the squeeze machine, I applied almost twice as much pressure as later. As I learned to accept the feeling of gentleness, too much pressure became most uncomfortable.

That night I wrote to Mother, telling her about my feeling of worthlessness, my fixation on the sliding glass door, and my inner conflict with the cattle chute. Was I just some weirdo with a crackpot idea?

Mother's letter came by return mail:

> . . . *Be proud you are different. All bright people who have contributed to life have been different and found the path of life lonely. While the joiners and social butterflies flutter about, Temple, you'll get real things done.*
>
> *And, dear, don't worry about the cattle chute. It is a "comfy." Remember when you were little you rejected all "comfies?" You*

couldn't bear them. Your need to turn to the
cattle chute now is natural. The hardest thing
in life is to unravel the unevenness of one's
mind. The part of you which is mature is
baffled by the immature side. Don't be
ashamed of early motivations. They are deep
in our fantasy life and part of the well spring
of life.

You need symbols. You love them. Like
a work of art they are a physical expres-
sion of what you feel. After all, all art is
symbolic . . .

A few days later I realized that I was suffering from
the same old syndrome—the lack of familiar surroundings, familiar students and teachers, familiar classes. I
wasn't worthless; I was simply reacting, as a typical
autistic individual, to a new environment, new people,
and new courses of study. I suffered terrible colitis attacks. I finally faced the fact that graduate school wasn't
the only way for me. I would try my hardest to get my
doctorate, but it wasn't worth jeopardizing my health. I'd
work and not fret. A statistic course wasn't what living
and learning was all about. I still occasionally got the
panicky feeling when I approached the supermarket's
sliding glass door. I finally decided that my ability to glide
through the glass sliding door would come for me
gradually—like understanding.

All that fall I struggled with the new challenges and
the old hang-up, the cattle chute. How could a device
which was often rough and harsh when used on cattle also
be used to generate gentleness and a caring spirit? I
thought about religion and how religious symbols
originated from violent and pagan rites. Even today,
though the original symbol has been modified, the emo-

tional impact is powerful. So it was with my cattle chute. The original machine exerted a powerful, submissive force. The newer model's force was gentle and by its gentleness exerted a greater strength through evoking caring emotions.

Someone asked me how I could love cats and at the same time perform scientific experiments on them. I couldn't answer. It was the same sort of question I'd asked myself about the origin of my cattle chute. How could a device that forced an animal to submit also be a device that generated love for fellow man?

CHAPTER TEN

Through the Sliding Glass Door

In February 1971 I went to the cattle feedlot and actually operated the cattle chute on 130 head of cattle. Previously I had only watched the cattle chute operation. On this occasion the three other workmen tolerated my presence because one worker was absent, and an extra hand was needed. The first time I worked the head gate improperly and the animal slipped through. The cattle were given the full treatment — branding, shots, castrating and I didn't freak out! I got right into the scene and acted as if I belonged there.

The feedlot cowboys had almost a childlike obliviousness concerning their work. They turned on the radio and kind of jigged as they worked to the click of the Spanish music.

I felt bad about the calf I had let slip through the head gate because then he had to be roped and dragged. The other three workers were tolerant of my mistake. One of them said, "Forget it. We all let one slip through

123

now and then. You're doing okay." By the end of the day I was giddy with self-satisfaction. My fellow workers complimented me on my quick learning. "You done good, Sis. You're some worker," one of the men said. I left the feedlot feeling confident in my abilities as a cattle chute operator and pleased with my ability to get along with fellow workers.

On my way back to the dorm I stopped at the supermarket. I walked through the sliding glass door. I did not cringe as the door glided open nor rush it as if a herd of cattle were behind me. I simply walked through like a normal person. I decided that getting along with people was like a sliding glass door. The door has to be approached slowly; it cannot be forced; otherwise, it will break. Relationships with people are the same way. If they are forced, the relationship doesn't work. One little shove can shatter everything. One bad word can spoil months of building up trust, respect, and confidence in another person.

That night I went to a psychology department party. After everyone had left, I had a long talk with the host. He said, "You seem different tonight, Temple. Even the other students noticed it."

"I'm no different."

"Well, you actually visited with your classmates. And you seemed interested in them."

"So?"

He cleared his throat. "So, that isn't your usual style."

"What is?"

He looked down at the floor a minute, then at me. "Well, to tell you the truth, you're considered by your classmates as a pretty unfeeling and uninvolved person. Some of your remarks in class would alienate a viper."

I wanted to say, "But that was before I became a cattle

chute operator and glided through the sliding glass door," but I didn't. He wouldn't have understood. I thanked him for the party and promised to try harder to be friendly. As I walked back to my room, I thought about what the host had said and it dawned on me—me, twenty-some years old—that I was different. In kindergarten I thought my *classmates* were different; in highschool I sometimes felt alienated as if I didn't quite fit in, but tonight for the first time I realized that I was really different. I was autistic. I was a special individual!

I continued working part-time as a cattle chute operator. At first, I wasn't too concerned about the cattle. Like many people in the industry, I looked upon them as commodities. But then, as I became more and more involved, my attitude changed. People, nice people, were sometimes cruel to the animals—prodding them, shocking them, beating them. This disturbed me. Later, I had the opportunity to go to work with a cattle chute equipment company selling chutes and feed wagons.

On one of my routes, I passed Beefland, the biggest slaughterhouse in the Southwest. I pulled to the side of the road and looked at the plant buildings. They were white, big, impressive. Having been reared in the East, I'd never been in a slaughterhouse before. I thought about the cattle I had handled in the cattle chute. They were being prepared for their final destiny at the great white plant. It all looked so neat—the white hospital-like building with a wooden ramp on one end, and trucks lined up at the loading docks at the other end. I felt as if I were circling Vatican City and trying to figure out a way to get in. As I looked at Beefland, I hoped that the animals would not be defiled at the slaughterhouse. I hoped that they would be allowed to die with dignity and walk up the ramp instead of being beaten or dragged. I wondered what really happened behind the white wall with all the machinery noises emanating from it. I decided that I had to get into that plant and see its operation. This decision became my new fixation. But it was not a symbolic fixation like the sliding glass door. Beefland was real. I had to face the thing all human beings fear — death — and try to find the meaning of life.

Finally I got to see the inside of Beefland, and I was surprised at my lack of reaction to it. The cattle just walked up the ramp, and bang! it was all over. Each animal was killed instantly with a device called a captive bolt stunner. This device drives a retractable bolt deep into the animal's brain and causes considerably less pain than the cattle suffers getting banged around in the cattle chute by rough cowboys during branding and vaccination.

At the end of my second year at graduate school I switched my major from psychology to animal science. From my enjoyment of horseback riding, to my interest in Aunt Ann's ranching, to cattle and cattle chutes, all my steps through life had seemed to lead toward this vocation. I was working part-time selling cattle chutes and visiting the cattle feedlots often. Changing my major to animal science seemed a natural.

It also seemed natural to make further improvements on my squeeze machine. After seeing hydraulically-operated cattle chutes at feedlots and gates at dairies that were operated by air cylinders, I decided to install such a device on my squeeze machine. Then the amount of pressure to be exerted could be controlled by pushing a lever while I was inside it. After studying about air-operated industrial equipment and learning some engineering principles, I installed an air cylinder and a control valve on the squeeze machine. This refinement made the machine much more relaxing and comforting. If the pressure was slowly released and then gradually increased, the soothing feeling melted away any barriers. At first, this frightened me. I felt vulnerable. I wrote in my diary: "Maybe it's the fear of opening a door and seeing what's on the other side. Once the door is opened and the sight seen, it can't be denied. Sometimes in the squeeze machine I feel like a wild animal afraid of being touched. At first I jerk away. But gradually I give in. This is the fourth major improvement on the squeeze machine. Each improvement melts away more of my wall of tactual defensiveness."

See Appendix C for details on squeeze machine design and operation.

Christmas 1973 I spent at Mother's house and suffered one of the worst nerve attacks in my life. One of the reasons was the old autistic syndrome—the lack of sameness in my environment. Another reason was the time of the year. The days were short. I had been living in Arizona, working in the stockyards, following my routine. Now, suddenly, different surroundings, happenings, routines. I figured out that Christmas holidays were stressful for several reasons: First, I was away from my own territory and had no control; I had to think about other people's needs almost exclusively; I was away from the things which most interested me, such as cattle, feedlots, and cattle chutes; I was away from my squeeze machine. Another factor was pride. I had had several articles published in our state farm magazine. Here in New York nobody had even heard of this respected journal. My efforts seemed minimized.

I talked with Mother and she suggested that I write down my thoughts—like a newspaper assignment—the subject being me. She said, "Temple, you have two choices. You can either take the easy way out and return to Arizona or you can stay until the 27th and complete the assignment."

I stayed. Perhaps some of my nervousness was caused by old memories. Mother gave me letters written to my psychiatrist when I was having trouble in school. It shook me to find out how really odd some of my behavior had been and how worried my parents were about me. From the letters I learned that my parents were concerned that I would not be able to lead a "normal" life.

Usually when visiting Mother in New York, I didn't bother to set up one of my old chutes, but as the holidays progressed, I became more and more stressed. All my energy seemed to be directed toward preventing a full-blown nerve attack. I was frightened because I felt as if I were regressing. I finally set up the old clunky chute and though it was extremely uncomfortable, (since it was one of the first models), it relieved some of my nervousness. To some people my chute was suspect, but for me it served two functions: First, it provided stimulation (a necessity for autistic kids) and confinement, which helped me relax; secondly, it provided a warm, soft comfortable environment which helped me receive and give affection.

After reading letters and evaluations of my past, I talked with Mother. I wanted to touch her, tell her she was special.

Another thing I realized after being "home" for seven days was how very important cattle, feedlots, and cattle chutes were for me, most of the things which made me feel as if somebody or something were missing here. I knew I was involved with cattle but until this trip home I never realized just how total my involvement was.

After the holidays I returned to Arizona and visited the feedlots and Beefland. I found that I was becoming more tuned in to the animals and their feelings of fear and anxiety. Today some meatpackers recognize that kind, humane treatment of the animals not only raises employees' morale and how they feel about themselves but also pays off in profits. Bruised meat cannot be used for human food, and the meat from stressed hogs is lower in quality.

I wrote in my diary: "I find that if I place my hands on an animal waiting in line at Beefland, I can feel its nervousness. Sometimes touching the animal calms it. Some people say that since they are going to be killed, being kind to them is not necessary. My answer to this is: what if your grandmother was in the hospital dying? How would you like it if the doctor said, 'She's just a terminal patient. We can throw her over in a corner.' "

When I returned to the feedlots, I found I could

operate the cattle chute on the animals more gently. Some cowboys would slam the gate on the animal's head and squeeze it too hard with a hydraulically operated chute. One kind cowboy, Allen, showed me how to get tuned into the cattle and to operate the chute quickly and gently without hurting the animals. A good operator can make the squeeze chute act like an extension of his hands. I found that if I relaxed when operating the chute, the cattle didn't jump around as much. Animals sense tension in people.

One day I operated the stunning pen at Beefland and killed about 20 cattle. I had mixed emotions on this part of my job and was rather unnerved. That night when I got home, I could not bring myself to say that I killed them. For a few minutes I felt like St. Peter at the gates of cattle heaven. But gradually I realized that to be an expert in the stunning pen was really the art of caring. Paradoxically, I was learning to care at the slaughterhouse.

The next year I worked for a large cattle equipment and construction company designing more humane equipment for slaughtering cattle. I won the contract for our company to install new ramps and equipment at Beefland. Building a "Stairway to Heaven" for the animals was more than just constructing a steel ramp-way into a concrete room. All of the workers, myself included, invested ourselves in the project. Sometimes tempers flared, but when the job was completed, we were better friends.

As the "stairway" began to take shape, many thoughts crowded in on me. I became aware of how precious life was. I thought about death and I felt close to God. He had given us dominion over the animals so we could make use of them, but I realized now, more than ever, that the animals were His creation, too, and, thus, they should be treated with respect.

One day my blind roommate visited the plant. She reached over the side of the chute and touched the cattle. She wrote the following prayer after her visit: "The 'Stairway to Heaven' is dedicated to persons who desire to learn the meaning of life and not to fear death. You, through respect for these animals, can come to respect your fellow man as well. Touch, Listen, and Remember."

I described my feelings about the cattle in my diary:

I reached over the side of the chute and touched a steer's back. I had empathy for the animal and maybe it sensed it because its fear diminished. In a few seconds the animal would become beef, and the essence of its individuality would return to God. For any living thing to continue to live another living thing has to die. I felt a closeness and a respect for the steer I had never felt before.

To become more aware and understand, not just in my intellect but in my heart, I realized that I would actually have to kill the animal. To refuse to participate in the killing part of the process would be a denial of reality. I was afraid to step over to the stunner's platform and kill the animal. There has been great progress made in the equipment used to kill food animals. It is easy to operate and painless for the animal.

People have a conscience which enables them to be aware of the consequences and meaning of their acts. The ending of the life of a living thing should be approached with respect. This would help me become more aware of the meaning of my own existence. To become aware I had to be able to kill the animals, but at the same time maintain an at-

titude of gentleness and respect for them.
Killing is a harsh act, but harshness is part of
nature; gentleness is also part of nature. If
you lose respect for the animals the killing
process degenerates into assembly line box
stapling, or you turn into a brute. On the
other hand many people run away from the
fact that the animals have to die.

A person who is able to respect the
animals and plants which we harvest for food
will be able to take the first step of learning
the meaning of life. A farmer is said to be
close to the earth. Many people in our
modern technological society have lost touch
with the earth. Their values have become
trivial . . .

I respected the cattle by touching them and thus reassuring them. Trainers of show cattle always touch an animal firmly. Studies report that a light touch has an alerting effect and firm pressure has a calming effect. Patients in a coma experience a reduction in blood pressure when touched by another human being. I have tamed cross-bred Brahman and Hereford calves by confining them in the squeeze chute and then petting them. Research on monkeys and pigs reveals that they will become quiet and inactive by stroking. Comforting tactile stimulation will raise endorphin levels in chicks. Tactile stimulation is not only reassuring to all children, but essential for the child who is autistic. Overcoming tactile defensiveness is like taming an animal. When the animal is first touched, it flinches and moves away. Gradually, it learns to accept and then enjoys being touched.

Gradually I, too, was experiencing more "normal" emotional ties to people. Lorna King asked me to take a seven-year-old autistic boy on a carnival ride since she knew that he and I shared enjoyment of the intense vestibular and tactile stimulation. Afterwards I wrote in my diary:

> *While I was on the ride with Jimmy, I totally forgot about being on the ride, and my concentration was focused on Jimmy to make sure he would not get scared. I put my arm around him and held him. I had cast my defenses aside, but after the ride I got a little shook up because I realized that my defenses had been penetrated. Going on the "Round Up" with Jimmy forced me to respond to a person — I was not just responding to the machine. If he had gotten scared, I was the only one he could turn to.*

What started out as just a fixation has turned into a life-long dedication of improving the welfare of farm animals by designing humane equipment and facilities. In the livestock industry the science of nutrition and genetics has advanced far beyond the science of animal behavior and handling.

In graduate school I did my master's thesis on the design of cattle chutes in feedlots. It was one of the first farm animal behavior research projects in the United States. My work on cattle behavior and handling is considered pioneering in my field. My college advisors, who were in the field of veterinary science and nutrition, thought that cattle behavior during handling was not a proper academic subject. My tendency to fixate was actually an advantage in this situation. It provided me with the motivation to pursue my interest. A certain amount of fixation is required to reach any goal. Otherwise, I could have said, "Oh, shucks. I'll do my thesis on something the professors want." The tendency to fixate is a normal human trait but autistics have that tendency to a much greater degree. Since writing that thesis, I have published over 100 papers and articles on livestock handling in both the professional and livestock industry trade press.

As an adult, I have overcome some autistic tendencies—I no longer hit people or "peep," but I still have deficit areas. When I went to Vienna to present a paper on livestock handling, I was frustrated by my inability to communicate in German. I found myself reverting to the simplified one-word speech I had used as a child. When I became lost in the foreign city, it was all I could do not to scream. I was under a great deal of stress and got shingles during the meeting. Shingles is a painful inflamation of the nerve endings which can be brought on by stress. It would seem that maturation might cloak autistic characteristics, but they are still there. Nevertheless, I presented my paper to scientists from throughout the world, and it received a special citation as one of the top four papers at the European Meeting of Meat Research Workers.

CHAPTER ELEVEN

Working—Coping—Surviving

My mind is completely visual, and spatial work such as drawing is easy. I have designed big steel and concrete livestock facilities, but remembering a phone number or adding up numbers in my head is difficult. If I have to remember an abstract concept, I "see" the page of the book or my notes in my mind and "read" information from it. Melodies are the only things I can memorize without a visual image. I remember very little of what I hear unless it is emotionally arousing or I can form a visual image. When I think about abstract concepts such as human relationships, I use visual similies—for example, relationships between people are like a sliding glass door that must be opened gently or it may shatter. Studies show that pictures could be used to effectively communicate with autistic children. Another study reports that autistics often process written language better than spoken. Even now I mix up similar sounding words such as "over" and "other" and misspell words such as "freight" and "receive." I also mix up right and left or clockwise and counter-clockwise until I make a motion with my hand.

It has been over ten years since I took a statistics course. When I tried, I failed the first exam. I was unable to hold one piece of information in my mind while I manipulated another piece of information. Translating the mathematical symbols and manipulating the equation at the same time was impossible.

Recently, as an adult, I had a series of tests to determine my abilities and handicaps. On the Hiskey Nebraska Spatial Reasoning test my performance was at the top of the norms. It was concluded that "the ceiling of this subtest is probably too low to access accurately her extraordinary spatial visualization ability." This test was untimed.

On the Woodcock-Johnson test, my performance in Spatial Relations was lower because it was a timed, high speed test. The items I solved were correct, but I did not finish enough items to get a superior score. The conclusion was, "She has a highly visual, synthetic mind, which can integrate a large amount of material visually and which tends to apprehend information as visual wholes."

When I design equipment, it takes time to form the visual image. The image gradually emerges while I draw. When the entire image is formed, I can place cattle and people in it and imagine how they will behave under different situations. I can rotate the image and make it move in my mind like a movie. I can't imagine what non-visual thinking would be like.

My scores on other Woodcock-Johnson tests were superior in Memory for Sentences, Picture Vocabulary, and Antonyms-Synonyms. I did reasonably well on Memory for Numbers because I figured out a way to beat the test. I repeated the numbers out loud.

My performance on the Blending subtest, identifying a word that was slowly sounded out at the rate of one syllable per second, was at the second grade level. The Visual Auditory Learning subtest, memorizing the meanings for arbitrary symbols such as ⊢ meaning horse and then translating such symbols into English, was also on the second grade level. The only symbols I could learn were ones where I could create a visual image such as a man riding a horse with a flag. Nouns were easier to learn than verbs.

On the Analysis Synthesis subtest, identifying equivalents for various combinations of colored squares, I scored at the fourth-grade level. This test required intense sustained concentration. I often have lapses in concentration, which has no effect on my ability to draw blueprints and design equipment, but which does make it extremely difficult to follow the sequence in a statistics lecture.

I was also on the fourth grade level in the Concept Formation subtest. This test required identification of the dimension or dimensions differentiating one set of colored shapes from another. I did poorly because I had to hold the concept in my short term memory while I looked at the cards to pick out the one that had the same concept. The problem was that I forgot the concept while I was looking for the answer. If I had been allowed to write down the concept, I think I would have performed much better.

The Visual Attention Span, a subtest from the Hiskey Nebraska, was another test on which I did poorly. It required looking at a series of pictures, then picking the original pictures from a large group of pictures, and placing them in the correct sequence. I was able to choose the correct pictures but I made errors in the sequence.

Another test that was difficult for me was the Oral

Directions, a subtest of the Detroit Tests of Learning Aptitude. This test provided a measure of concentration combined with short term recall of a sequence. It required recall of a series of directions to write or draw with a pencil on specified figures on the test form. This task required retaining information in short term memory while concentrating and performing the action. When I receive directions from a gasoline station, I have to write them down if there are more than three roads or turns in the sequence. My difficulties on many of the subtests stemmed from my inability to hold one piece of information in my mind while I manipulated another piece of information. I have many dyslexic traits: difficulty with sequential memory and foreign language, mixing up words like revolution and resolution or over and other, and using visual strategies of recall.

But visual thinking is an asset for an equipment designer. I am able to "see" how all the parts of a project will fit together and also see potential problems. Sometimes a sequential thinker makes a mistake in designing because he can't see the whole. Designing a piece of equipment with a sequential mind may be just as difficult for an engineer as statistic equations are for me. Many times in industry I have seen a brilliant maintenance man with a high school education design a piece of equipment after all the PhD engineers had failed. Sometimes engineers make mistakes which seem obvious to me. There may be two basic kinds of thinking—visual and sequential. Society needs to recognize the value of people who think visually. Studies by the Educational Testing Service indicate that high school students twenty years ago scored higher on the ability to visualize three dimensional objects. Thomas Hilton, senior researcher at ETS, states that today's potential engineers and architects may not be as well qualified as those who emerged from

Blueprint by the author

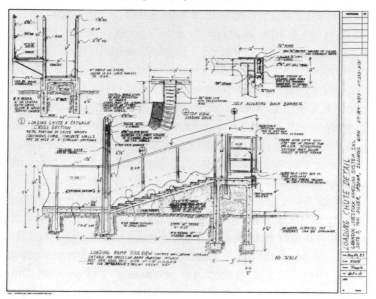

Aerial photo of cattle handling system designed by the author at John Wayne's feedlot.

high school two decades ago. Misinterpretation of psychological test results could label a brilliant visual thinker as below average in intelligence. Einstein was a visual thinker who failed his high school language requirement and relied on visual methods of study. A recent study states that people with delayed left hemisphere growth have talents. If autism and dyslexia were ultimately prevented, maybe the price would be turning potentially talented individuals into ones with mediocre talents.

For example, autopsies of brains from dyslexics indicate that left cortex development is impaired, and neurons have grown in the wrong direction. Impairment on the left side could allow the right side of the brain to develop larger neural circuits. Albert Galaburda from the Harvard Medical School concludes: "Such a system could help explain the anecdotal evidence suggesting that among dyslexics there is a disproportionately large number of individuals with special talents in music, visual-spatial abilities and left-handedness."

The ability to visualize may explain why some dyslexics become top executives in corporations. They have an overall vision and direct their businesses as an integrated whole, instead of being involved in details.

Like dyslexics, autistics may also have a left brain hemisphere defect. CAT scans at Yale University detected left hemisphere deficiencies in some autistic children.

Research with artificial intelligence may provide some insights. Until recently all computers used sequential methods to solve problems. At the national Conference on Artificial Intelligence, the "Boltzmann machine" was described. This computer has a massively parallel organization. The circuits work in parallel rather than sequentially. Visual thinking and processing of information through many parallel circuits may be similar. In a recent review of the literature Deborah Fein and her colleagues in Boston concluded that the "neurological impairments in autism may be both more diffuse and pervasive and more variable from case to case than presently theorized." This could explain why treatments which work with one autistic child may not work with another. The parts of the brain that are damaged may vary greatly from case to case.

I am no longer driven by my nerves. The drug (generic name, Imipramine) Tofranil (50 mg a day) controls them. I learned about the Tofranil treatment from an article in *Psychology Today* by P.H. Wender and D.F. Klein. Imipramine adjusts my metabolism and reduces the sensitivity of my central nervous system to incoming sensory input. Tofranil reduces the sensitivity of B-adrenergic receptors in the brain. The receptors are part of the intricate neuronal circuits in the brain that process sensory input. Reducing the sensitivity of these receptors in the part of the brain called the locus ceruleus reduces the effects of sensory input on the brain. It is like adjusting the idle screw on a car's carburetor. Before taking the drug, the engine was racing all the time. Now the engine runs at a normal speed.

Recent studies reveal that many people with "panic anxiety" attacks can be successfully treated with antidepressants. It is also likely that the tendency toward panic anxiety may be inherited.

Gone are the frenzied searches for the basic meanings of life. I no longer fixate on one thing since I am no longer driven. During the last four years I have written very few entries in my diary because the anti-depressant has taken away much of the fervor. With the passion subdued, my career and livestock equipment design business is going well. Since I am more relaxed, I get along better with people and stress-related health problems, such as colitis, are gone. Yet if medication had been prescribed for me in my early twenties, I might not have accomplished as much as I have. The "nerves" and the fixations were great motivators until they tore my body apart with stress-related health problems. Autistic and dyslexic traits are probably normal traits that become excessive in certain individuals. A certain amount of anxiety and fixation is needed to motivate a person to get things done.

Today I am successful in my business. I travel all over the United States, Europe, Canada, and Australia designing livestock handling facilities for ranches, feedlots and meatpacking plants. My experiences have given me empathy for the animals going through the facilities and help me to design better equipment. For instance, the chutes and pens that I design are round. The reason for this design is because cattle will follow a curved path more easily. There are two reasons for this: first, the cattle can't see what is at the other end and become frightened and, secondly, the curved equipment takes advantage of the animal's natural circling behavior. The principle is to work with the animal's behavior instead of against it. I think the same principle applies to autistic children—work with them instead of against them. Discover their hidden talents and develop them. I am also working on a doctorate at the University of Illinois in Animal Science. My thesis project is based on the effect of environmental enrichment on the behavior and central nervous system development of animals. Ongoing research at the university by W.T. Greenough and his associates indicates that the brain is very plastic and responsive to stimulation from the environment. Even an adult brain constantly grows new neural circuits and connections in response to stimulation.

As you can see, I have put a great deal of time and effort into learning about the neurology of autism—not only to understand myself better, but also to help put my experiences into a scientific perspective that might be helpful to others. In the last few years I've been a speaker at several workshops designed to help therapists, parents, and teachers of autistic children. After one of these, my friend Lorna King, who was also a speaker, wrote me:

Dear Temple:

As I listened to your lecture last week in Chicago, I couldn't help thinking back to the first time I heard you talk 12 years ago in Phoenix at a meeting of the local Society for Autistic Children. Even though the group was small, you were obviously very nervous and "up-tight." Your speech seemed pressured, coming in almost explosive bursts. You held yourself rigidly erect and were visibly very uncomfortable when someone insisted on shaking your hand.

What a contrast with your speech in Chicago! You seemed quite at ease and sprinkled your talk with humor, which the audience really appreciated. You handled questions easily, rubbed shoulders with the crowd during breaks, shook hands without hesitation, and generally seemed calm and self-assured.

Your old tendency to perseverate seems to be gone. You used to have a lot of trouble dropping one subject and going on to another—and I know that even though you were aware of it, you couldn't help it. Now that seems to be a thing of the past.

How wonderful that you are continuing to grow and develop. You are an inspiration to the rest of us to try to do the same!

Her letter reminded me of a recent article I had read in the paper about a "hands off" policy now in effect in nurseries, schools, and other institutions for children. I understand the reason—child molestation is a heinous crime—but there must be a balance. How ridiculous and unrewarding for a teacher to congratulate a child on a task well-done by saying, "Pat yourself on the back." All children need tactile stimulation—autistic children just need more.

CHAPTER TWELVE

Autistics and the Real World

You have read my story and have seen how I moved from my series of symbolic doors into the real world. But what does it mean to you, the parent or the professional who is deeply concerned and involved with childhood autism?

• First, like all children, no two autistic children are alike. What may work successfully for one will not work for another. It is true there are specific principles of learning that run through all human endeavors. The goal is to observe and find the specific pattern of responses each child exhibits, then move from there.

• Look for what interests your child and captures his fancy. If, for example he stands by the toilet, flushing it all day long, ask yourself, is it the sound, is it the pushing of the handle, or is it the cause and effect relationship that fascinates him? Take that involvement and divert it into other channels.

• As a child, I loved being spun. The Rotor ride at the carnival became an obsession with me and I stayed on it for hours. There is now evidence that, if there is not a history of epileptic seizures, spinning is an aid to the inner ear (vestibular) mechanism that assists balance, coordination, and perception. Admonition: Spinning to the point of nausea is not the goal. Inducing nystagmus (the flickering of the eye as the body regains its balance) is the goal.

• I also think that the squeeze machine could help some autistic children overcome their tactile defensiveness so that they would allow people to touch them and receive their affection. If the autistic child can learn to accept affection, this, in turn, might help him to learn to care about other people. The lack of empathy reported in some cases of high functioning autistics could be avoided. The squeeze machine and other deep pressure stimulation used in sensory integration therapy may calm an over-aroused nervous system and reduce hyperactivity. There are sensory integration specialists trained in the methods developed by A. Jean Ayres.

• Be a cautious observer. Watch not only for what the child is attracted to in motor responses (such as continual flushing of a toilet) but also for what bothers the child. Like many autistic children I could not stand loud noises. I could not stand a hefty hug. I felt as if I were being suffocated. And yet I loved putting things together — like building a replica of the Distorted Room.

• Often professionals will say things like, "Oh, no. Billy doesn't do that! (or can't do that). I tested him two years ago." That was two years ago. Not today. Findings, testing, observations need to be frequently carried out on a regular basis. Children, including the autistics, are not static.

- Encourage the autistic child to use his kinesthetic senses as in motor learning and educating the musculature of the body. My tactile senses were overly sensitive—tactually defensive. But my kinesthetic senses were wide open for learning. The sense of touch is a primary learning source. It should be used more not only with autistic children but with all children. Let the child use various textures and materials—woolens, sandpaper, clay, silks—for learning and let him trace, for example, in clay and wet sand. Musical and rhythmic activities are highly recommended for autistic children. Non-verbal autistics can sometimes sing words that they are unable to speak.

- All of us need a private place. Autistic children need their secret places, too, in which they can hide and retreat to their own world. After all, autistic is a "within-ness" disability, and autistic children need the security of their own hideaways. I had mine and it was a place for me to think and recharge myself.

- Be cautious in introducing pets to the autistic child. Because of perceptual disorganization, mistreatment of a pet is not unusual. First, give the child a soft, furry stuffed animal to pet and stroke. When the child clearly understands about taking care of that animal, introduce a real pet. Let the child hold it and stroke it. There is more and more evidence that pets can greatly aid in therapy, not only for the autistic, but for the elderly and infirm.

- Behavior modification techniques are another method of working with autistics. But one of the difficulties of this technique is that autistics, as a rule, have problems in generalizing a task. For instance, an autistic child learns to use a spoon to eat ice cream. Will he then transfer this learning ability to using a spoon for soup? Often an autistic can do one task but cannot convert that new skill to other tasks. Take each task, one by one, and treat it as a new task. But be aware. When generalization takes place, your child is moving closer to reality.

- Be aware of spontaneous reaction. When I threw books at other children, I reacted without thinking. Scolding an autistic child may lead to new improvement or changes in behavior, but most often the child has virtually no control over such reactions.

- Watch food intake. The body requires a nutritional stability to stay on an even keel. And often the autistic does not have the inner mechanisms to produce and process what is needed. Trace minerals contribute to the stability (homeostasis) of the body. Many autistic children have a deficiency of zinc and, according to Allan Cott, MD, sometimes overloadings of copper—both of them vital trace minerals in the body's blood and immune system. To find out if there is a lack of zinc (which is critically important to the inner ear development, the vestibular responses), see an orthomolecular specialist who will administer an eight-hour glucose tolerance test. Perhaps megavitamin therapy is needed. Bernard Rimland, at the Institute for Child Behavior Research in San Diego, has completed several studies in which vitamin B6 and magnesium have been found helpful to many autistic children. Other researchers have confirmed his findings. The child should also be evaluated for allergies. Try these methods before resorting to drugs.

- Many autistics have serious food allergies. Behavior sometimes improves when allergic foods are removed from the child's diet. Some common foods that may cause allergy problems are: milk, wheat, corn, tomatoes, chocolate, sugar, and mushrooms. Seek out a specialist who is knowledgeable in the effects of food allergies on behavior.

- Mary Coleman, MD, in Washington, D.C. is

researching metabolic defects in autism. Certain types of autism may possibly benefit from special diets that correct the metabolic defect.

• Be careful not to load a child up on too many drugs. When drugs work, they are really great. Tofranil is a miracle medicine for me, but it may be awful for someone else. Overdosing youngsters with drugs can be dangerous. My personal bias is to avoid drugs in children as long as possible and then use them only as a last resort. When drugs are called for, use one drug at a time and carefully evaluate its effect. If more than one drug is given simultaneously, it is difficult to evaluate the effect. Giving a child medication often just masks a symptom, but finding the right drug which actually corrects or compensates for faulty biochemistry is very useful. Once a successful drug is found, use the smallest effective dose.

• Maintain a stable, ordered, secure environment. The autistic child simply cannot function if there are too many daily changes. Do things each day in sequence. Starting at the beginning of the day — first we get up, then we wash, then we eat breakfast, and so on. The autistic child is unable to bring order to his world. You must provide that order in his environment. Autistics might march to a different beat but that beat can be meaningful.

• What do autistic children hear? Sometimes I heard and understood and other times sounds or speech reached my brain like the unbearable noise of an onrushing freight train. Noise and confusion at large gatherings of people overwhelmed my senses. Monitor what you say to the autistic child. Keep your sentences short and simple. Look directly at the child because the autistic learns to read the whole body — not just the words. If necessary, grasp the chin of the child and make eye contact. This is so difficult for autistic children. Their eyes seem to see everything except the one who is speaking to them. Be dramatic in your talking. Let your child read happiness through your smile or unhappiness through a down-turned mouth. These facial expressions will do much to draw the child's eyes to your eyes, face, and body. Don't speak in a monotone and do emphasize key words as in "What a *nice* bunny you drew!"

• As to fixations, channel them into positive actions. Singleness of purpose (persistence) can work wonders. High functioning autistic adults, who are able to live independently and keep a job, often have work that is in the same field of interest as their childhood fixations. One man with a childhood fixation on numbers today works successfully doing fiscal efficiency reports.

• Seek out specialists. Get various opinions. Join your local associations for disabled children. Keep up on what is going on—the new methods, treatments, research. And absolutely talk with other parents.

Today I am a successful designer of livestock equipment with my own company. Who would have thought it of that "weirdo"? I look at the invitation to the class reunion again. I think I will go. After all, with the help and love of family and others, I have come a long way—a very, very long way. With my ability for visual thinking, I "see" others "labeled autistic" gliding through their symbolic doors to their own successes.

Appendix A

Institute for Child Behavior Research
4182 Adams Ave.
San Diego, CA 92116
(619) 281-7165

INFORMATION AND REPORT SHEET
Diagnostic Check List for Behavior-Disturbed Children: Form E-2

1. The Form E-2 Diagnostic Check List is intended to differentiate cases of early infantile autism (EIA, also known as classical autism, or Kanner's syndrome) from the wider range of children who are called "autistic," "childhood schizophrenic," "autistic-like," etc. Only about ten per cent of the children loosely described as "autistic" or "autistic-like" fit into the closely defined EIA syndrome described by Leo Kanner in 1943.

2. Form E-2 was designed for completion by the child's parents. Since in many instances the behavioral patterns of children with autism and similar disorders begin to change rather markedly after the fifth birthday, all of the questions on Form E-2 pertain to the child's behavior and appearance, medical history, etc. from birth to age 6. The child's behavior after age six is much less diagnostic.

3. Form E-2 is to be used to identify cases of EIA primarily for the purposes of *biological research;* i.e. research on biochemistry, cytogenetics, EEG's, drugs, etc. In biological research, it is extremely important that the *exact* diagnosis of the child is known. Differentiating Kanner's syndrome cases from the broader range of autistic cases is of interest primarily to researchers, since certain metabolic differences have been found between Kanner's syndrome and other types of autism (e.g. 1, 2, 4).

4. Form E-2 is NOT designed to determine whether or not a child is autistic for the purposes of being admitted to an educational or rehabilitational program. Special education will benefit virtually *all* of the children described as autistic, schizophrenic, etc., and thus Form E-2 is not a valid instrument for use in qualifying or excluding children from school programs.

5. As of February, 1980, the Institute for Child Behavior Research had in its files completed checklists for over 6,700 children, from 40 countries. The majority of these forms have been sent to us directly by parents to facilitate our research. The rest were received from more than 400 collaborating professionals to whom ICBR sends E-2 score reports for the cases they submit.

6. To determine if a child is a classical case of infantile autism, Form E-2 is scored as though it were a test (3). One *plus* (+) point is accrued for each question (sign or symptom) characteristic of EIA, and one *minus* (−) is accrued for each question answered in the non-EIA direction. The child's total "score" is the difference between his EIA (+) and non-EIA (−) scores. Three scores are derived:

   a) *Autistic Behavior Score:* indicates the degree to which the child's behavior resembles that of the child with classical EIA. Behavior scores range from − 35 to + 40.

   b) *Speech Score:* indicates the degree to which the child's speech pattern resembles that of the child with classical EIA. A score of + 6 or higher on the speech score indicates that the child's speech closely resembles that of the Kanner-type child. Mute children (about half of all autistic children are mute) receive a score near zero on the speech scale. Speech scores range from − 10 to + 14.

   c. *Total Score:* the sum of the speech and behavior scores. Any score above + 20 indicates the child is very probably a case of classical EIA. *Only about 10 per cent of the children called "autistic" have total scores above + 20.* Several studies have shown that there are important biochemical differences between children who score above + 20 and those who score in the lower range. It is for the purpose of facilitating such research that the E-2 Diagnostic Check List was developed. Total scores range from − 40 to + 45.

A low or minus score on any of the three scales means that the child's pattern of speech and behavior is dissimilar from that of the child with classical EIA. It does *not* mean that the child is not "autistic" as the word autistic is usually used, or that the child is not qualified for or entitled to a school program designed for autistic children.

7. At a later time, when sufficient resources are available, it is planned to do an extensive computer analysis of Form E2 data bank, to provide detailed information about each child for whom an E-2 Form has been submitted to this Institute. We expect that a sophisticated computer pattern analysis program (several are being considered) will permit us to classify the remaining 90 per cent of "autistic" children—those who are not cases of classical Kanner Syndrome—into small meaningful homogeneous subgroups for study by biologically-oriented researchers. Such subgrouping will be of great help to research scientists in the future. When this work is completed, ICBR will report the results on all cases in our files to the parents or professionals who submitted them.

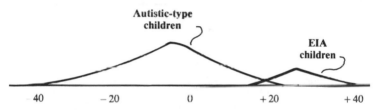

FIG. 1. Frequency distribution of total "autism" scores is derived from Form E-2. Overlapping curves depict hypothetical separation of true autistic cases from distribution of scores of autistic-type children.

REFERENCES

1. Boullin, D., M. Coleman, R. O'Brien. "Abnormalities in Platelet 5-Hydroxytryptamine Efflux in Patients With Infantile Autism." *Nature, 226,* 1970, 371-372.

2. Boullin, D., M. Coleman, R. O'Brien, B. Rimland. "Laboratory Predictions of Infantile Autism Based on 5-Hydroxytryptamine Efflux From Blood Platelets and Their Correlation With the Rimland E-2 Score." *Journal of Autism and Childhood Schizophrenia, 1,* 1971, 63-71.

3. Rimland, B. "The Differentiation of Childhood Psychoses: An Analysis of Checklists for 2,218 Psychotic Children." *Journal of Autism and Childhood Schizophrenia, 1,* 1971, 161-174.

4. Rimland, B. "Platelet Uptake and Efflux of Serotonin in Subtypes of Psychotic Children." *Journal of Autism and Childhood Schizophrenia, 6,* 1976, 379-382.

			E-2 Score	
Name	ICBR No.	Behavior	Speech	Total
Temple Grandin	_7298_	_+13_	_-4_	_+9_

ICBR Publication No. 38   **February 1980**

Diagnostic Check List for Behavior-Disturbed Children
(Form E-2)

(Before Marriage) _____

Has this child been diagnosed before? _____

  If so, what was diagnosis _____

Diagnosed by: _____

Where? _____

Instructions: You are being asked to fill out this questionnaire concerning your child in order to provide research information which will be helpful in learning more about the causes and types of behavior disturbances in children. Please pick the one answer you think is most accurate for each question. If you want to comment or add something about a question, add it right next to the question, if there is room. Or circle the number of the question, copy the number on the back of the questionnaire and write your comment there. Your additional comments are welcome, but even if you do add comments, please mark the printed question as well as you can. Remember, pick just one answer, and mark it with an "X," for each question.

  It would be helpful if, on a separate sheet, you would write in any information about the child and his sisters or brothers which you think may be significant. (For example: Twins, living or dead; Behavior problems; IQ scores, if known.)

USE AN "X" TO MARK ONE ANSWER FOR EACH QUESTION. DO NOT SKIP MAIN QUESTIONS. SUB-QUESTIONS (NOT ALONG LEFT MARGIN) MAY BE SKIPPED.

*Note: This Check List is designed primarily for children 3 to 5 years old. If child is over 5, answer as well as you can by recall of the child's behavior.

1. Present age of child:
   - _X_ 1. Under 3 years old
   - ____2. Between 3 and 4 years old
   - ____3. Between 4 and 5 years old
   - ____4. *Between 5 and 6 years old
   - ____5. *Over 6 years old (Age:_____years)

2. Indicate child's sex:
   - ____1. Boy
   - _X_ 2. Girl

3. Child's birth order and number of mother's other children:
   - ____1. Child is an only child
   - _X_ 2. Child is first born of _4_ children
   - ____3. Child is last born of ____ children
   - ____4. Child is middle born; ____ children are older and ____ are younger than this child
   - ____5. Foster child, or don't know.

4. Were pregnancy and delivery normal?
   - _X_ 1. Pregnancy and delivery both normal
   - ____2. Problems during both pregnancy and delivery
   - ____3. Pregnancy troubled, routine delivery
   - ____4. Pregnancy untroubled; problems during delivery
   - ____5. Don't know

5. Was the birth premature (birth weight under 5 lbs)?
   - ____1. Yes (about ____ weeks early; ____ lbs)
   - _X_ 2. No
   - ____3. Don't know

6. Was the child given oxygen in the first week?
   - ____1. Yes
   - _X_ 2. No
   - ____3. Don't know

7. Appearance of child during first few weeks after birth:
   - ____1. Pale, delicate looking
   - ____2. Unusually healthy looking
   - _X_ 3. Average, don't know, or other

8. Unusual conditions of birth and infancy (check only one number in left-hand column):
   - ____1. Unusual conditions (Indicate which: blindness ____, cerebral palsy ____, birth injury ____, seizures ____, blue baby ____, very high fever ____, jaundice ____, other _____
   - ____2. Twin birth (identical ____, fraternal ____)

155

_____3. Both 1 and 2
__X_4. Normal, or don't know

9. Concerning baby's health in first 3 months:
   __X_1. Excellent health, no problems
   _____2. Respiration (frequent infections ____, other _____)
   _____3. Skin (rashes ____, infection ____, allergy ____,
           other _____)
   _____4. Feeding (learning to suck ____, colic ____, vomiting
           ____, other _____)
   _____5. Elimination (diarrhea ____, constipation ____, other
           _____)
   _____6. Several of above (indicate which: 2 ____, 3____,
           4 ____, 5 ____, 6 ____)

10. Has the child been given an electroencephalogram (EEG)?
    __X_1. Yes, it was considered normal
    _____2. Yes, it was considered borderline
    _____3. Yes, it was considered abnormal
    _____4. No, or don't know, or don't know results

11. In the first year, did the child react to bright lights, bright col-
    ors, unusual sounds, etc.?
    _____1. Unusually strong reaction (pleasure ____, dislike
            ____).
    _____2. Unusually unresponsive
    __X_3. Average, or don't know

12. Did the child behave normally for a time before his abnormal
    behavior began?
    _____1. Never was a period of normal behavior
    __X_2. Normal during first 6 months
    _____3. Normal during first year
    _____4. Normal during first 1½ years
    _____5. Normal during first 2 years
    _____6. Normal during first 3 years
    _____7. Normal during first 4-5 years

13. (Age 4-8 months) Did the child reach out or prepare himself to
    be picked up when mother approached him?
    _____1. Yes, or I believe so
    _____2. No, I don't think he did
    __X_3. No, definitely not
    _____4. Don't know

14. Did the child rock in his crib as a baby?
    _____1. Yes, quite a lot
    _____2. Yes, sometimes

_____3. No, or very little

__X__4. Don't know

15. At what age did the child learn to walk alone?
_____1. 8-12 months
__X__2. 13-15 months
_____3. 16-18 months
_____4. 19-24 months
_____5. 25-36 months
_____6. 37 months or later, or does not walk alone

16. Which describes the change from crawling to walking?
__X__1. Normal change from crawling to walking
_____2. Little or no crawling, gradual start of walking
_____3. Little or no crawling, sudden start of walking
_____4. Prolonged crawling, sudden start of walking
_____5. Prolonged crawling, gradual start of walking
___ 6. Other, or don't know

17. During the child's first year, did he seem to be unusually intelligent?
_____1. Suspected high intelligence
__X__2. Suspected average intelligence
_____3. Child looked somewhat dull

18. During the child's first 2 years, did he like to be held?
_____1. Liked being picked up; enjoyed being held
_____2. Limp and passive on being held
__X__3. You could pick child up and hold it only when and how it preferred
_____4. Notably stiff and awkward to hold
_____5. Don't know

19. Before age 3, did the child ever imitate another person?
_____1. Yes, waved bye-bye
_____2. Yes, played pat-a-cake
_____3. Yes, other (_____)
_____4. Two or more of above (which? 1 _____, 2 _____, 3 _____)
__X__5. No, or not sure

20. Before age 3, did the child have an unusually good memory?
_____1. Remarkable memory for songs, rhymes, TV commercials, etc., in words
_____2. Remarkable memory for songs, music (humming only)
_____3. Remarkable memory for names, places, routes, etc.
__X__4. No evidence for remarkable memory

157

_____5. Apparently rather poor memory
_____6. Both 1 and 3
_____7. Both 2 and 3

21. Did you ever suspect the child was very nearly deaf?
    _X_1. Yes
    _____2. No

22. (Age 2-4) Is child "deaf" to some sounds but hears others?
    _X_1. Yes, can be "deaf" to loud sounds, but hear low ones
    _____2. No, this is not true of him

23. (Age 2-4) Does child hold his hands in strange postures?
    _X_1. Yes, sometimes or often
    _____2. No

24. (Age 2-4) Does child engage in rhythmic or rocking activity for very long periods of time (like on rocking-horse or chair, jump-chair, swing, etc.)?
    _X_1. Yes, this is typical
    _____2. Seldom does this
    _____3. Not true of him

25. (Age 2-4) Does the child ever "look through" or "walk through" people, as though they weren't there?
    _X_1. Yes, often
    _____2. Yes, I think so
    _____3. No, doesn't do this

26. (Age 2-5) Does child have any unusual cravings for things to eat or chew on?
    _____1. Yes, salt or salty foods
    _____2. Yes, often chews metal objects
    _____3. Yes, other (_____)
    _____4. Yes, more than 2 above (which? _____)
    _X_5. No, or not sure

27. (Age 2-4) Does the child have certain eating oddities such as refusing to drink from a transparent container, eating only hot (or cold) food, eating only one or two foods, etc.?
    _____1. Yes, definitely
    _X_2. No, or not to any marked degree
    _____3. Don't know

28. Would you describe your child around age 3 or 4 as often seeming "in a shell," or so distant and "lost in thought" that you couldn't reach him?
    _X_1. Yes, this is a very accurate description

       ____2. Once in a while he might possibly be like that

       ____3. Not an accurate description

29. (Age 2-5) Is he cuddly?
       ____1. Definitely, likes to cling to adults
       ____2. Above average (likes to be held)
       _X_ 3. No, rather stiff and awkward to hold
       ____4. Don't know

30. (Age 3-5) Does the child deliberately hit his own head?
       _X_ 1. Never, or rarely
       ____2. Yes, usually by slapping it with his hand
       ____3. Yes, usually by banging it against someone else's legs or head
       ____4. Yes, usually by hitting walls, floor, furniture, etc.
       ____5. Several of above (which? 2 ____, 3 ____, 4 ____)

31. (Age 3-5) How well physically coordinated is the child (running, walking, balancing, climbing)?
       ____1. Unusually graceful
       _X_ 2. About average
       ____3. Somewhat below average, or poor

32. (Age 3-5) Does the child sometimes whirl himself like a top?
       ____1. Yes, does this often
       _X_ 2. Yes, sometimes
       ____3. Yes, if you start him out
       ____4. No, he shows no tendency to whirl

33. (Age 3-5) How skillful is the child in doing fine work with his fingers or playing with small objects?
       _X_ 1. Exceptionally skillful
       ____2. Average for age
       ____3. A little awkward, or very awkward
       ____4. Don't know

34. (Age 3-5) Does the child like to spin things like jar lids, coins, or coasters?
       _X_ 1. Yes, often and for rather long periods
       ____2. Very seldom, or never

35. (Age 3-5) Does child show an unusual degree of skill (much better than normal child his age) at any of the following:
       ____1. Assembling jig saw or similar puzzles
       ____2. Arithmetic computation
       ____3. Can tell day of week a certain date will fall on
       ____4. Perfect musical pitch
       ____5. Throwing and/or catching a ball

X 6. Other (*drawing - painting - crafts*)
___7. More than one of above (which? _____)
___8. No unusual skill, or not sure

36. (Age 3-5) Does the child sometimes jump up and down gleefully when pleased?
___1. Yes, this is typical
___2. No or rarely

37. (Age 3-5) Does child sometimes line things up in precise evenly-spaced rows and insist they not be disturbed?
___1. No
_X_2. Yes
___3. Not sure

38. (Age 3-5) Does the child refuse to use his hands for an extended period of time?
___1. Yes
_X_2. No

39. Was there a time before age 5 when the child strongly insisted on listening to music on records?
___1. Yes, insisted on only certain records
___2. Yes, but almost any record would do
___3. Liked to listen, but didn't demand to
_X_4. No special interest in records

40. (Age 3-5) How interested is the child in mechanical objects such as the stove or vacuum cleaner?
___1. Little or no interest
___2. Average interest
_X_3. Fascinated by certain mechanical things

41. (Age 3-5) How does child usually react to being interrupted in what he is doing?
___1. Rarely or never gets upset
_X_2. Sometimes gets mildly upset; rarely very upset
___3. Typically gets very upset

42. (Age 3-5) Will the child readily accept new articles of clothing (shoes, coats, etc.)?
___1. Usually resists new clothes
_X_2. Doesn't seem to mind, or enjoys them

43. (Age 3-5) Is child upset by certain things that are not "right" (like crack in wall, spot on rug, books leaning in bookcase, broken rung on chair, pipe held and not smoked)?
___1. Not especially

    _X_ 2. Yes, such things often upset him greatly

    _____ 3. Not sure

44. (Age 3-5) Does child adopt complicated "rituals" which make him very upset if not followed (like putting many dolls to bed in a certain order, taking exactly the same route between two places, dressing according to a precise pattern, or insisting that only certain words be used in a given situation)?

    _____ 1. Yes, definitely

    _X_ 2. Not sure

    _____ 3. No

45. (Age 3-5) Does child get very upset if certain things he is used to are changed (like furniture or toy arrangement, or certain doors which must be left open or shut)?

    _____ 1. No

    _____ 2. Yes, definitely

    _X_ 3. Slightly true

46. (Age 3-5) Is the child destructive?

    _X_ 1. Yes, this is definitely a problem

    _____ 2. Not deliberately or severely destructive

    _____ 3. Not especially destructive

47. (Age 3-5) Is the child unusually physically pliable (can be led easily; melts into your arms)?

    _____ 1. Yes

    _____ 2. Seems normal in this way

    _X_ 3. Definitely not pliable

48. (Age 3-5) Which single description, or combination of two descriptions, best characterizes the child?

    _____ 1. Hyperactive, constantly moving, changes quickly from one thing to another

    _____ 2. Watches television quietly for long periods

    _____ 3. Sits for long periods, staring into space or playing repetitively with objects, without apparent purpose

    _____ 4. Combination of 1 and 2

    _____ 5. Combination of 2 and 3

    _X_ 6. Combination of 1 and 3

        _1-3_

49. (Age 2-5) Does the child seem to want to be liked?

    _____ 1. Yes, unusually so

    _____ 2. Just normally so

    _X_ 3. Indifferent to being liked; happiest when left alone

50. (Age 3-5) Is child sensitive and/or affectionate?

    _X_ 1. Is sensitive to criticism and affectionate

    _____ 2. Is sensitive to criticism, not affectionate

_____3. Not sensitive to criticism, is affectionate
_____4. Not sensitive to criticism nor affectionate

51. (Age 3-5) Is it possible to direct child's attention to an object some distance away or out a window?
    _X_1. Yes, no special problem
    _____2. He rarely sees things very far out of reach
    _____3. He examines things with fingers and mouth only

52. (Age 3-5) Do people consider the child especially attractive?
    _X_1. Yes, very good-looking child
    _____2. No, just average
    _____3. Faulty in physical appearance

53. (Age 3-5) Does the child look up at people (meet their eyes) when they are talking to him?
    _X_1. Never, or rarely
    _____2. Only with parents
    _____3. Usually does

54. (Age 3-5) Does the child take an adult by the wrist to use adult's hand (to open door, get cookies, turn on TV, etc.)?
    _X_1. Yes, this is typical
    _____2. Perhaps, or rarely
    _____3. No

55. (Age 3-5) Which set of terms best describes the child?
    _X_1. Confused, self concerned, perplexed, dependent, worried
    _____2. Aloof, indifferent, self-contented, remote

56. (Age 3 and 5) Is the child extremely fearful?
    _____1. Yes, of strangers or certain people
    _X_2. Yes, of certain animals, noises or objects
    _____3. Yes, of 1 and 2 above
    _____4. Only normal fearfulness
    _X_5. Seems unusually bold and free of fear _in undertaking what interests her_
    _____6. Child ignores or is unaware of fearsome objects

57. (Age 3-5) Does he fall or get hurt in running or climbing?
    _____1. Tends toward falling or injury
    _____2. Average in this way
    _____3. Never, or almost never, exposes self to falling
    _X_4. Surprisingly safe despite active climbing, swimming, etc. – _very true_

58. (Age 3-5) Is there a problem in that the child hits, pinches, bites or otherwise injures himself or others?
    _____1. Yes, self only

162

___X_2. Yes, others only — mosTly in Temper-unTrusTworthy
_____3. Yes, self and others   with small animals
_____4. No (not a problem)

59. At what age did the child say his first words (even if later
    stopped talking)?
    _____1. Has never used words
    _____2. 8-12 months
    _____3. 13-15 months
    _____4. 16-24 months
    _____5. 2 years-3 years
    __X_6. 3 years-4 years
    _____7. After 4 years old
    _____8. Don't know

59a. On lines below list child's first six words (as well as you can
     remember them)
     _____
     _____

60. (Before age 5) Did the child start to talk, then become silent
    again for a week or more?
    _____1. Yes, but later talked again (age stopped _____, dura-
            tion _____)
    _____2. Yes, but never started again (age stopped _____)
    __X_3. No, continued to talk, or never began talking

61. (Before age 5) Did the child start to talk, then stop, and begin to
    whisper instead, for a week or more?
    _____1. Yes, but later talked again (age stopped _____, dura-
            tion _____)
    _____2. Yes, still only whispers (age stopped talking _____)
    ____3. Now doesn't even whisper (stopped talk _____;
            stopped whisp _____)
    __X_4. No, continued to talk, or never began talking

62. (Age 1-5) How well could the child pronounce his first words
    when learning to speak, and how well could he pronounce dif-
    ficult words between 3 and 5?
    _____1. Too little speech to tell, or other answer
    _____2. Average or below average pronunciation of first
            words ("wabbit," etc.), and also poor at 3 to 5
    _____3. Average or below on first words, unusually good at
            3-5
    _____4. Unusually good on first words, average or below at
            3-5
    _____5. Unusually good on first words, and also at 3-5

63. (Age 3-5) Is the child's vocabulary (the number of things he can

163

name or point to accurately) greatly out of proportion to his ability to "communicate" (to answer quetions or tell you something)?

    _____1. He can point to many objects I name, but doesn't speak or "communicate"

    _____2. He can correctly name many objects, but not "communicate"

    _X__3. Ability to "communicate" is pretty good — about what you would expect from the number of words he knows

    _____4. Doesn't use or understand words

64. When the child spoke his first sentences, did he surprise you by using words he had not used individually before?

    _____1. Yes (Any examples? _____)

    _X__2. No

    _____3. Not sure

    _____4. Too little speech to tell

65. How did child refer to himself on first learning to talk?

    _____1. "(John) fall down," or "Baby (or Boy) fall down."

    _X__2. "Me fall down," or "I fall down"

    _____3. "(He, Him, She, or Her) fall down"

    _____4. "You fall down"

    _____5. Any combination of 1, 2, and/or 3

    _____6. Combination of 1 and 4

    _____7. No speech or too little speech as yet

66. (Age 3-5) Does child repeat phrases or sentences that he has heard in the past (maybe using a hollow, parrot-like voice), what is said having little or no relation to the situation?

    _____1. Yes, definitely, except voice not hollow or parrot-like

    _____2. Yes, definitely, including peculiar voice tone

    _____3. Not sure

    _____4. No

    _X__5. Too little speech to tell

67. (~~Before~~ By age 5) Can the child answer a simple question like "What is your first name?" "Why did Mommy spank Billy?"

    _X__1. Yes, can answer such questions adequately

    _____2. No, uses speech, but can't answer questions

    _____3. Too little speech to tell

68. (Before age 5) Can the child understand what you say to him, judging from his ability to follow instructions or answer you?

    _X__1. Yes, understands very well

    _____2. Yes, understands fairly well

    _____3. Understands a little, if you repeat and repeat

    _____4. Very little or no understanding

69. (Before age 5) If the child talks, do you feel he understands what he is saying?
  ____1. Doesn't talk enough to tell
  ____2. No, he is just repeating what he has heard with hardly any understanding
  ____3. Not just repeating — he understands what he is saying, but not well
  __X_4. No doubt that he understands what he is saying ⟶ qeƚs
      frosTraTed if you don'T undersTand

70. (Before age 5) Has the child used the word "Yes"?
  __X_1. Has used "Yes" fairly often and correctly
  ____2. Seldom has used "Yes," but has used it
  ____3. Has used sentences, but hasn't used word "Yes"
  ____4. Has used a number of other words or phrases, but hasn't used word "yes"
  ____5. Has no speech, or too little speech to tell

71. (Age 3-5) Does the child typically say "Yes" by repeating the same question he has been asked? (Example: You ask "Shall we go for a walk, Honey?" and he indicates he does want to go by saying "Shall we go for a walk, Honey?" or "Shall we go for a walk?")
  ____1. Yes, definitely, does not say "yes" directly
  ____2. No, would say "Yes" or "OK" or similar answer
  ____3. Not sure
  ____4. Too little speech to say

72. (Before age 5) Has the child asked for something by using the same sentence you would use when you offer it to him? (Example: The child wants milk, so he says: "Do you want some milk?" or "You want some milk")
  ____1. Yes, definitely (uses "You" instead of "I")
  ____2. No, would ask differently
  ____3. Not sure
  ____4. Not enough speech to tell

73. (Before age 5) Has the child used the word "I"?
  ____1. Has used "I" fairly often and correctly
  ____2. Seldom has used "I," but has used it correctly
  ____3. Has used sentences, but hasn't used the word "I"
  ____4. Has used a number of words or phrases, but hasn't used the word "I"
  ____5. Has used "I", but only where word "you" belonged
  ____6. Has no speech, or too little speech to tell

74. (Before age 5) How does the child usually say "No" or refuse something?
  ____1. He would just say "No"
  ____2. He would ignore you

165

    ____3. He would grunt and wave his arms
    _X_4. He would use some rigid meaningful phrase (like "Don't want it!" or "No milk!" or "No walk!")
    ____5. Would use phrase having only private meaning like "Daddy go in car"
    ____6. Other, or too little speech to tell

75. (Before age 5) Has the child used one word or idea as a substitute for another, for a prolonged time? (Example: always says "catsup" to mean "red", or uses "penny" for "drawer" after seeing pennies in a desk drawer)

    ____1. Yes, definitely
    ____2. No
    _X_3. Not sure
    ____4. Too little speech to tell

76. Knowing what you do now, at what age do you think you could have first detected the child's abnormal behavior? That is, when did detectable abnormal behavior actually begin? (Under "A", indicate when you might have; under "B" when you did.

A		B
____1. In first 3 months		_____
____2. 4-6 months		_____
_X_3. 7-12 months		_____
____4. 13-24 months		__X__
____5. 2 years-3 years		_____
____6. 3 years-4 years		_____
____7. After 4th year		_____

Parents' highest educational level (77 for father, 78 for mother)

77.   78.

77	78
5	*5*

1. Did not graduate high school
2. High school graduate
3. Post high school tech. training
4. Some college
5. College graduate
6. Some graduate work
7. Graduate degree (_____)

79. Indicate the child's nearest blood relatives, including parents, who have been in a mental hospital or who were known to have been seriously mentally ill or retarded. Consider parents, siblings, grandparents, uncles and aunts.
If none, check here ☐

166

	Relationship		Diagnosis (if known)		
___1.	_____	Schizophrenia___	Depressive___	Other___	
___2.	_____	___	___	___	
___3.	_____	___	___	___	
___4.	_____	___	___	___	
✓ 5.	great uncle	✓	___	___	

FORM E2, PART 2

Please answer the following questions by writing "*1*" if *Very True,* "*2*" if *True* and *3* if *False* on the line preceding the question. Except for the first two questions, which pertain to the child before age 2, answer "Very True" (1) or "True" (2) if the statement described the child any time before his 10th birthday. If the statement is not particularly true of the child before age 10, answer "False" (3). Remember: 1 = Very True, 2 = True, 3 = False.

80. _2_ Before age 2, arched back and bent head back, when held
81. _1_ Before age 2, struggled against being held
82. _3_ Abnormal craving for certain foods
83. _3_ Eats unusually large amounts of food
84. _2_ Covers ears at many sounds
85. _1_ Only certain sounds seem painful to him
86. _3_ Fails to blink at bright lights
87. _2_ Skin color lighter or darker than others in family (which: lighter _X_, darker ___)
88. _1_ Prefers inanimate (nonliving) things
89. _1_ Avoids people
90. _3_ Insists on keeping certain object with him
91. _3_ Always frightened or very anxious
92. _3_ Inconsolable crying
93. _1_ Notices changes or imperfections and tries to correct them
94. _3_ Tidy (neat, avoids messy things)
95. _3_ Has collected a particular thing (toy horses, bits of glass, etc.)
96. ____ After delay, repeats *phrases* he has heard
97. ____ After delay, repeats *whole sentences* he has heard
98. ____ Repeats *questions* or *conversations* he has heard, over and over, without variation
99. _1_ Gets "hooked" or fixated on one topic (like cars, maps, death)

100. _3_ Examines surfaces with fingers
101. _1_ Holds bizarre pose or posture
102. _3_ Chews or swallows nonfood objects
103. _1_ Dislikes being touched or held
104. _1_ Intensely aware of odors
105. _2_ Hides skill or knowledge, so you are surprised later on
106. _2_ Seems not to feel pain
107. _3_ Terrified at unusual happenings
108. _3_ Learned words useless to himself
109. _3_ Learned certain words, then stopped using them

Use the rest of this sheet for supplying additional information that you think may lead to understanding the cause or diagnosis of the child's illness.

Appendix B
General Information
(Revised May 1993)

The primary source of information about autism and the primary referral service for families with autistic children is the Autism Society of America. It was founded in 1965 by parents and professionals with the support and backing of Dr. Bernard Rimland. Its 7000 individual members and 200 local chapters are dedicated to the education and welfare of persons with autism and related disorders of communication and behavior. It runs an information and referral service, publishes a newsletter, "The Advocate," and maintains a mail order bookstore. For further information contact Autism Society of America, 8601 Georgia Avenue, Suite 503, Silver Spring, Maryland 20910 (301) 565-0433.

You can write ASA for their full booklist at the above address. Another helpful source for materials on autism is the Autism Research Institute, 4182 Adams Avenue, San Diego, CA 92116 which will send a list of publications on request.

Selected References.

Ayres, J.A. 1979. *Sensory Integration and the Child.* Western Psychological Services, Los Angeles.

Banion, D.O., Armstrong, B., Cummings, R.A. and Strange, J. 1978. Disruptive behavior: A dietary approach. *Journal of Autism and Developmental Disorders,* Vol. 8, pp. 325.

Barrett, R.P., Feinstein, C. and Hole, W.T. 1988/1989. Effects of Naloxone and Naltrexone on self-injury. *American Journal of Mental Retardation,* (In Press).

Bauman, M.L. 1991. Microscopic neuroanatomic abnormalities in autism. *Pediatrics,* Vol. 87, Part 2, pp. 791-796.

Bhatara, V., Clark, D.L., Arnold, L.E., Gunsett, R. and Smeltzer, D.J. 1981. Hyperkinesis treated with vestibular stimulation: An exploratory study. *Biological Psychiatry,* Vol. 16, pp. 269-279.

Bemporad, J.R. 1979. Adult recollections of a formerly autistic child. *Journal of Autism and Developmental Disorders,* Vol. 9. pp. 179-197.

Casler, L. 1965. Effects of extra tactile stimulation on a group of institutionalized infants. *Genetic Psychology Monographs,* Vol. 71, pp. 137-175.

Ceci, S. 1985. Horse sense: Not intelligence. A short report by Nick Jordan. *Psychology Today,* February, p. 20.

Cesaroni, L. and Garber, M. 1991. Exploring the experience of autism through first hand accounts. *Journal of Autism and Developmental Disorders,* Vol. 21, pp. 303-312.

Charney, D.S., Heninger, G.R. and Breier, A. 1984. Noradrenegeric function in panic anxiety. *Archives of General Psychiatry,* Vol. 41, pp. 751-764.

Coleman, M. and Gilberg, C. 1986. *The Biology of the Autistic Syndrome.* Praeger Publishers.

Condon, W. 1981. Asyncrony. *Omni,* December, p. 18. Reported by Walli Leff.

Cook, E.H., Rowlett, R., Jaselskis, C. and Leventhal, B. 1992. Fluoxetine (Prozac) treatment of children and adults with autistic disorder and mental retardation. *Journal of the American Academy of Child and Adolescent Psychiatry,* Vol. 31, pp. 739-745.

Courchesne, E. et al. 1988. Hypoplasia of cerebellar vermal lobules VI and VII in autism. *New England Journal of Medicine,* Vol. 318, pp. 1349-1354.

Dantzer, R. and Mormede, P. 1983. De-arousal properties of stereotyped behavior. Evidence from pituatary adrenal correlations in pigs. *Applied Animal Ethology,* Vol. 10, pp. 233-243.

Favell, J.E., McGimsey, J.F. and Jones, M.L. 1978. The use of physical restraint in the treatment of self-injury and as positive reinforcement. *Journal of Applied Behavior Analysis,* Vol. 11, pp. 225-241.

Foley, J.P. 1938. Tonic immobility in the rhesus monkey (Macaca Mulatta) induced by manipulation, immobilization and experimental inversion of the visual field. *Journal of Comparative Psychology,* Vol. 26, pp. 515-526.

Fox, M.W. 1971. *Integrative Development of the Brain and Behavior in the Dog.* University of Chicago Press, Chicago.

Galaburda, A. 1983. Developmental dyslexia: Current anatomical research. *Annals of Dyslexia,* Vol. 33, pp. 41-53. Orton Dyslexia Society, Baltimore, Maryland.

Gajzago, C. and Prior, M. 1974. Two cases of "recovery" in Kanner's Syndrome. *Archives of General Psychiatry,* Vol. 31, pp. 264-268.

Gedye, A. 1989. Episodic rage and aggression attributed to frontal lobe siezures. *Journal of Mental Deficiency Research,* Vol. 33, pp. 369-379.

Geschwind, N. and Galaburda, A. 1985. Cerebral lateralization. *Archives of Neurology,* Vol. 42, pp. 428-459.

Gillberg, C., Terenius, L. and Lonnerholm, G. 1985. Endorphin activity in childhood psychosis. *Archives of General Psychiatry,* Vol 42, pp. 780-783.

Grandin, T. 1992. Calming effects of deep touch pressure in patients with autistic disorder, college students and animals. *Journal of Child and Adolescent Psychopharmacology,* Vol. 2, pp. 63-70.

Grandin, T. 1992. An inside view of autism. In E. Schopler and G.B. Mesibov (Eds.) *High Functioning Individuals with Autism.* Plenum Press, New York, pp. 105-126.

Grandin, T. 1980. Observations of cattle behavior applied to the design of cattle handling facilities. *Applied Animal Ethology,* Vol. 6, pp. 19-31.

Greenough, W.T. and Juraska, J.M. 1979. Experience induced changes in fine brain structure: Their behavioral implications. In M.E. Hahn, C. Jensen and B.C. Dudek, (Eds.), *Development and Evolution of Brain Size: Behavioral Implications.* Academic Press, New York, pp. 295-320.

Harlow, H.F. and Zimmerman, R.R. 1959. Affectional responses in the infant monkey. *Science,* Vol. 130, pp. 421-432.

Hersher, L. 1985. The effectiveness of behavior modification on hyperkinesis. *Child Psychology and Human Development,* Vol. 16, pp. 87-96.

Kanner, L. 1943. Autistic disturbances of affective contact. *Nervous Child,* Vol. 2, pp. 217-250. Reprinted in A.E. Donnelan (Ed.), Classic Readings in Autism, 1985, Teachers College Press, Columbia University, New York.

Kanner, L. 1971. Follow-up study of eleven autistic children originally reported in 1943. *Journal of Autism and Childhood Schizophrenia,* Vol. 1, pp. 112-145.

Kumazawa, T. 1963. "Deactivation" of the rabbit's brain by pressure application to the skin. *Electroencephalography and Clinical Neurophysiology,* Vol. 15, pp. 660-671.

LaVigna, G.W. and Donnellan, A.M. *Alternatives to Punishment.* Irvington Publishers, New York.

Landa, R., Piven, J. and Wzorek, M.M. et al. 1992. Social language use in parents of autistic individuals. *Psychological Medicine,* Vol. 22, pp. 245-254.

Lovaas, I. 1987. Behavioral treatment and normal educational and intellectual functioning in young autistic children. *Journal of Consulting and Clinical Psychology,* Vol. 55, pp. 3-9.

Marcuse, F.L. and Moore, A.U. 1944. Tantrum behavior in the pig. *Journal of Comparative Psychology.* Vol. 37, pp. 235-241.

Martineau, J., Barthelemy, C., Garreau, B. and Lelord, G. 1985. Vitamin B6, magnesium and combined B6-Mg. Therapeutic effects in childhood autism. *Biological Psychiatry,* Vol. 20, pp. 467-478.

McCray, G.M. 1978. Excessive masturbation in childhood: A symptom of tactile deprivation. *Pediatrics,* Vol. 62, pp. 277-279.

McDougal, C.J., Price, L.H., Volkmar, F.R. et al. 1992. Clomipramine in autism preliminary evidence of efficacy. *Journal of the Academy of Child and Adolescent Psychiatry,* Vol. 31, pp. 746-750.

171

McGee, J.J. et al. 1987. *Gentle teaching.* Human Sciences Press, New York.

McGimsey, J.F. and Favell, J.E. 1988. The effects of increased physical exercise on disruptive behavior in retarded persons. *Journal of Autism and Developmental Disorders,* Vol. 18, pp. 167-179.

Melzack, R. and Burns, S.K. 1965. Neurophysiological effects of early sensory restriction. *Experimental Neurology,* Vol. 13, pp. 163-175.

Murphy, G. 1982. Sensory reinforcement in the mentally handicapped and autistic child, a review. *Journal of Autism and Developmental Disorders,* Vol. 12, pp. 265-278.

O'Connell, T.S. 1974. The musical life of an autistic boy. *Journal of Autism and Childhood Schizophrenia,* Vol. 4, pp. 223-229.

Ornitz, E.M. 1985. Neurophysiology of infantile autism. *Journal of the Academy of Child Psychiatry,* Vol. 24, pp. 251-262.

Panksepp, J. 1979. A neurochemical theory of autism. *Trends in Neurosciences,* July, pp. 174-177.

Powers, M.D. and Thorwarth, C.A. 1985. Effect of negative reinforcement on tolerance of physical contact in a preschool child. *Journal of Clinical Psychology,* Vol. 14, No. 4, pp. 299-303.

Rapoport, J.L. 1989. *The Boy Who Couldn't Stop Washing,* E.P. Dutton, New York.

Ratey, J.J. et al. 1987. Autism: The treatment of aggressive behaviors. *Journal of Clinical Psychopharmacology,* Vol. 7, No. 1, pp. 35-41.

Rausch, P.B. 1981. Effects of tactile and kinesthetic stimulation on premature infants. *JOGN Nursing* (January/February) pp. 34-37.

Ray, T.C., King, L.J. and Grandin, T. 1988. The effectiveness of self-initiated vestibular stimulation in producing speech sounds in an autistic child. *Journal of Occupational Therapy Research,* Vol. 8, pp. 186-190.

Rimland, B. 1964. *Infantile Autism.* Appleton Century Crofts, New York.

Rumsey, J.M., Duara, R., Grady, C., Rapoport, J.L., Margolin, R.A., Rappoport, S.I. and Cutler, N.R. 1985. Brain metabolism in autism. *Archives of General Psychiatry,* Vol. 42, pp. 448-455.

Sakai, K.K., Ary, T.E., Hymson, D.L. and Shapiro, R. 1979. Effect of cuddling on the body temperature and cyclic nucleotides in the CFS of the cat. *Experimental Brain Research,* Vol. 34, pp. 379-382.

Schrieber, H., Bell, R., Wood, G., Carlson, R., Wright, L., Kufner, M. and Villescas, R. 1978. Early handling and maternal behavior: Effect on d-Amphetamine responsiveness in rats. *Biochemistry and Behavior,* Vol. 9, pp. 785-789.

172

Sheehan, D.V., Beh, M.B., Ballenger, J. and Jacobsen, G. 1980. Treatment of endogeneous anxiety with phobic, hysterical and hypochondriacal symptoms. *Archives of General Phychiatry,* Vol. 37, pp. 51-59.

Simons, D. and Land, P. 1987. *Nature,* Vol. 236, pp. 694 (Rat whisker experiment).

Simons, J.M. 1974. Observations on compulsive behavior in autism. *Journal of Autism and Childhood Schizophrenia,* Vol. 4, pp. 1-10.

Stehi, A. 1991. *Sound of a Miracle.* Doubleday, New York.

Sullivan, R.C. 1980. Why do autistic children . . . ? *Journal of Autism and Developmental Disorders,* Vol. 10, pp. 231-241.

Takagi, K. and Kobagasi, S. 1956. Skin pressure reflex. *Acta Medica et Biologica,* Vol. 4, pp. 31-37.

Volkmar, F.R. and Cohen, D.J. 1985. The experience of infantile autism: A first person account by Tony W. *Journal of Developmental Disorders,* Vol. 15, pp. 47-54.

Williams, D. 1992. *Nobody Nowhere.* Times Books, New York.

Wing, L. 1976. *Early Childhood Autism.* 2nd Edition, Pergamon Press, New York.

Young, G.L., Kavanaugh, M.E., Anderson, G.M., Shaywitz, B.A. and Cohen, D.D. 1982. Clinical neurochemistry of autism and related disorders. *Journal of Autism and Developmental Disorders,* Vol. 12, pp. 147-165.

Zentall, S.S. and Zentall, T.R. 1983. Optimal stimulation: A model for disordered activity and performance in normal and deviant children. *Psychological Bulletin,* Vol. 94, pp. 446-471.

Zisserman, L. 1992. The effects of deep pressure on self stimulating behaviors in a child with autism and other disabilities. *American Journal of Occupational Therapy,* Vol 46, pp. 547-551.

Technical Appendix C

(Revised May 1993)

This appendix contains technical information that will be helpful to parents, teachers and other professionals who are treating a child or adult with autism.

Cause of Autism

Most cases of autism are caused by a complex inheritance of many interacting genetic factors. There is a continuum from normal to abnormal. Autistic traits often show up in a mild degree in the parents, siblings and close relatives of an autistic child. Some of the traits that seem to be associated with autism are: intellectual giftedness, shyness, learning disabilities, depression, anxiety, panic attacks, Tourettes (tic disorder) and alcoholism. Possibly a small amount of these traits confers an advantage, such as high intelligence or creativity, while too many will cause problems. Other causes of autism are the Fragile X gene, insults to the fetus such as rubella or other viruses, and very high fevers at a young age.

Brain autopsy research and MRI studies both indicate that people with autism have structural abnormalities in the brain. Certain areas of the brain such as the limbic system and the cerebellum are immature. Some of the pioneering research in this area has been done by Margaret Bauman at Massachusetts General Hospital in Boston, Massachusetts, and Eric Courchesne in San Diego, California. Other studies have shown that people with autism have abnormally slow transmission of nerve impulses through the brain stem. In summary, autism is a disorder where some parts of the brain are underdeveloped and immature but other parts of the brain possibly may be more developed. This may partly explain the enhanced visual and savant skills in some people with autism.

Autism Subtypes

Dr. Bauman's research shows that the underlying brain abnormalities are similar between different types of autism. However, different autism subtypes will respond differently to different treatments. For example, a drug that works on one type will be worthless on another. This also is true for educational, behavioral and sensory treatments. A treatment that works well for one subtype may be terrible for another. In my book, I recommend grasping the child's chin to force eye contact. This method helped me to stop tuning out and withdrawing. A somewhat intrusive therapist or teacher prevented me from retreating into a world of rocking and stereotypic behavior.

Donna Williams, author of *Nobody Nowhere,* explained to me that this treatment would have been too overwhelming for her and would have caused her to withdraw even further. Her sensory processing problems are much more severe than mine. Whereas I was overly sensitive to sound and touch, Donna sometimes has sensations from the ears and eyes that merge together. Incoming sensation becomes a meaningless jumble when she becomes excited. She can handle input from only one sensory channel at a time. If she is concentrating on listening to speech, she is unable to recognize a cat when it jumps on her. If she attends to the cat, speech perception is blocked. She also has problems determining where her body boundary is located.

Dr. Gedye in British Columbia, Canada, has discovered that some aggressive outbursts are caused by small epileptic seizures, which are very difficult to detect on an EEG machine. Some of the sensory jumbling that occurs in the more severe forms of autism may be caused by miniature seizures that are due to a lack of mylinization of the neurons. Sensory processing problems may be due to immature brain development.

Autistic subtypes can range from the classical type described by Kanner to the so-called low functioning type. I prefer the term regressive epileptic. These children are often normal until 18 to 24 months and then lose their speech. As one moves away from the Kanner type and towards the regressive epileptic side of the continuum, sensory processing problems become worse. Whereas I had normal ability to hear speech, some more severely afflicted people with autism may hear speech as a jumble of sound. The regressive epileptic types also are more likely to have easily detectable epileptic seizures and movement (motor) disorders. Some of these people are retarded but others are not. Emotions and affect may tend to become less rigid and more normal as one moves away from the Kanner end of the continuum.

Treatment and Education

Early intervention and placement of a child into a good educational program will improve the prognosis for all types of autism. A good program should use a variety of treatment methods because each child is different. There is a tendency for some autism professionals to claim that only their program will work. I have observed that effective teachers use the same methods regardless of theoretical orientation. Good teachers or or therapists are worth their weight in gold. Treatment for sensory oversensitivity and sensory processing problems should be made available to all students. An occupational therapist is recommended for sensory integration therapy. Auditory training can help reduce sound sensitivity and problems with static or buzzing sounds in the ears. For more information contact the Georgianna Organization in Westport, Connecticut. Vigorous exercise also will help calm the nervous system and reduce aggressive and hyperactive behavior.

An observant teacher or parent can determine if a bad behavior has a behavioral cause or a biological cause. A child may attempt to break the telephone to prevent the bell from ringing. Fear of a noise that hurts the ears can be the cause of many tantrums. However, many autistic children learn that they can manipulate adults by throwing tantrums. When this occurs, the use of behavior modification can work wonders. If a child spits, keep on teaching. If you stop teaching you have rewarded bad behavior. Some inappropriate behaviors are an attempt to communicate. Try to determine what triggers bad behavior.

Autistic children and adults are visual learners who think in visual images. Typewriters and word processors should be introduced at an early age. Avoid long strings of verbal information. If a child can read, provide written instructions. Typewriters may help severely afflicted individuals communicate.

Tactile Stimulation

Animal studies have shown that neurochemical changes occur immediately in response to comforting petting. The autistic child's failure to enjoy comforting tactile stimulation may be one cause of neurochemical abnormalities. If placement of an isolation-reared monkey in a social environment corrects abnormal neurochemistry, then it would be logical to theorize that neurochemical abnormalities caused by a lack of comforting tactile stimulation could be corrected by getting the child to accept comforting touching. In autistic infants, tactile stimulation such as stroking and cuddling may promote more normal development. Even if the baby is indifferent to being cuddled, it may still be beneficial. If the baby resists being touched, it would need to be gradually "trained" to tolerate comforting touching.

The original fetal defect in brain development is probably responsible for the baby's avoidance of being touched and comforted. The longer a baby lives without experiencing the feeling of being comforted, the more likely the brain circuits involved in the development of emotional contact with people will be damaged. Numerous animal studies have shown that brain circuits which are constantly used will become larger. Circuits which are used will be retained and enlarged whereas circuits which are idle will shrink. If the baby does not use his "feeling" circuits, they may shrivel up. Many people believe that connections between brain cells cannot grow in adults. Animal research has shown that dendrites, the branches between nerve cells, still grow and form connections in adults.

Squeeze Machine

Possibly the squeeze machine would be helpful in inducing older autistic children and adults to accept being touched, reduce hyperactivity, and nervous system over-arousal. Clinical observations have indicated that comforting tactile stimulation will reduce hyperactivity, and autistics enjoy it. The following is a more complete description of the squeeze machine.

The squeeze machine is completely lined with thick, foam rubber covered with plastic cloth-backed upholstery material. It squeezes the user very firmly, yet is soothing and comforting. The padding is designed to conform to the user's body so there are no uneven pressure points. The feeling of the pressure is all encompassing and creates an environment that is soothing. At the same time the brain is receiving large amounts of input from the pressure. Pressure applied by the machine activates pressure receptors from every nerve branch from the spinal cord.

Once the user is held by the squeeze machine, he cannot pull away or stiffen up to avoid the feeling of being held. It is extremely important that the user has control over the machine. He must be able to operate the controls and be able to release the pressure at any time. After a person has been in the machine for about 10 to 15 minutes at a constant pressure, the soothing effect will wear off as the tactile system becomes habituated. To maintain the soothing comforting effect, the user should very slowly release the pressure and then very slowly increase it back to a level that feels comforting.

The squeeze machine has two foam rubber padded panels which are hinged at the bottom to form a V shape (see diagram). The user gets in between the two panels in the hands the hands and knees position. The squeeze pressure is applied along both sides of the body when the panels are pulled together at the top. The machine is powered by an air compressor which operates an air cylinder attached to the panels via pulleys. Since the machine is air powered, it will apply a constant pressure even if the user shifts position. The user's body is completely supported by the V shape, which enables the user to completely relax.

The machine also has a padded headrest and neck opening which is covered with soft flannel or acrylic fur. The neck opening provides a place against which the person can lean his shoulders. When the neck opening is closed around the neck, it enhances the feeling of being contained by the embrace of the squeeze.

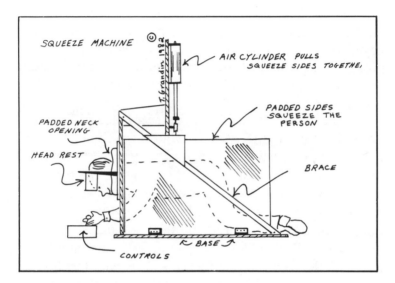

Stereotyped Behavior and Fixations

Earlier in this book I have made several references to animal studies which indicated that stereotyped behaviors have a calming effect on the nervous system. Robert Dantzer, one of the experts in this field, asked the following question at a scientific meeting: If the main purpose of stereotyped behavior is to calm the animal, why does the stereotyped behavior continue after the animal has calmed down? It is highly probable that stereotyped behavior is pleasurable and becomes self-reinforcing. Animals which engage in stereotyped behavior have increased levels of endorphins. They may be experiencing a self-induced "high."

The longer a stereotyped behavior persists, the more ingrained it becomes in the connections between neurons (nerve cells). Stereotypes which have persisted for many years are difficult to stop. It is like a brook finding a new path. After a while, the brook digs a channel and becomes difficult to divert. The stereotyped behavior may become "burned" into the circuitry of the brain.

Many times I have stated that fixations should be directed into constructive channels. Parents, teachers, and therapists should work with fixations and not against them. There is an important difference between fixations and stereotyped behavior. Stereotyped behavior is monotonous, repetitive, and rhythmic and is not goal-directed. It follows a preset rigid pattern which is internally generated. Examples of stereotyped behavior in children are rocking and hand flapping. Examples in animals are pacing continuously around the same path or standing in one place and weaving.

True stereotyped behavior is probably very bad for the nervous system. To stop a stereotyped behavior, it must be *replaced* with some type of external stimulation. One must differentiate between stimulus seeking and stereotyped behavior. If the child rolls himself up tightly in a blanket, this is usually stimulus seeking and not stereotyped behavior. Providing deep pressure stimulation that a child seeks may help reduce stereotyped behavior. A vibrator applied to the head or hands will often stop self-injurious behavior.

A fixation is an interest which is external, such as vacuum cleaners, radios, maps, television commercials, et cetera. Autistic children who have recovered took their childhood fixations and directed them towards constructive goals. The most successful recoveries had a dedicated friend who helped them direct their fixations.

In his original paper in 1943 Kanner described eleven cases of Kanner's Syndrome. In 1971 he followed up his original eleven cases to see what had happened to them. There were six failures, two unknowns, one partial recovery, and two successes. The most successful of the recoveries works as a bank teller. The farmer who raised him found goals for his fixations.

Fixations can be directed into academics. If a child is fixated on vacuum cleaners, use a vacuum cleaner instruction book to teach reading. Scientific principles about electricity can be taught by getting the child interested in how the motor works.

The eleven Kanner cases were very similar when first diagnosed but the prognosis greatly varied from case to case. Children sent to large institutions all regressed and never recovered. Autistic children who are mainstreamed with normal children and have dedicated teachers will probably have a better prognosis.

Medications

About half of the people with autism can benefit from medications and the other half do not need them. Medications should be used very sparingly in young children. If a medication works it should provide fairly dramatic improvements in behavior. It should never be used to sedate a person. People on the regressive epileptic end of the autism continuum tend to respond best to beta blockers (blood pressure medication), vitamin B_6 and magnesium supplements, and anticonvulsant drugs such as Depakene, Depakote and Prednisone. The food supplement DMG, which can be bought at a health food store, also is helpful. Other useful drugs are Buspar and Naltrexone. Dr. Rowland Barrett and Carl Feinstein have found that short courses of the endorphin blocking drug Naltrexone greatly reduced self-injurious behavior. Prozac may prevent self injury.

People on the Kanner end of the spectrum, like myself, have responded very well to antidepressants such as Tofranil, Norpramin, Prozac or Anafranil. I have been on the same low 50 mg. of Norpramin dose for eleven years. The effective doses for people with autism are much lower than the doses recommended for treating depression. Too high a dose will cause insomnia, aggression and restlessness. If these symptoms occur the dose must be *lowered*. Some people respond well to two 20 mg. Prozac pills taken twice a week.

After a person has been on an antidepressant drug for several weeks or months the effect may wear off. If this occurs do *not* raise the dose. Continue with the same dose until the anxiety relapse subsides. I have had several reoccurences of anxiety. I stayed on the same 50 mg. dose and the drug started to work again after two to six weeks. Increasing the dose will cause serious problems with side effects.

Conclusion

People treating autistic children should avoid falling into the trap of using just one type of treatment. A variety of methods used together would probably be the most successful. I have visited many autism programs for young children. Effective programs often use many of the same procedures even though the theoretical orientation is different. The most successful programs start treatment by age three or four and provide contact with normal children. They are also very intense. Passive approaches do not work. A good program should also have flexible nonaversive behavior modification, sensory treatment, speech therapy, exercise, and music therapy.

Treatment and therapy should be started when abnormal behavior is first observed. The most important component of the treatment plan is the presence of loving people to work with the child. I recovered because my mother, Aunt Ann, and Bill Carlock cared enough about me to work with me.

. . . Temple Grandin